BASICS

DESIGN

GRIDS FOR GRAPHIC DESIGNERS

3rd edition

BLOOMSBURY VISUAL ARTS

LONDON · NEW YORK · OXFORD · NEW DELHI · SYDNEY

BLOOMSBURY VISUAL ARTS
Bloomsbury Publishing Plc
50 Bedford Square, London, WC1B 3DP, UK
1385 Broadway, New York, NY 10018, USA

BLOOMSBURY, BLOOMSBURY VISUAL ARTS and the Diana logo are trademarks
of Bloomsbury Publishing Plc

First published in Great Britain in 2012, by AVA Publishing SA
This edition published in Great Britain in 2021, by Bloomsbury Visual Arts
Copyright © Bloomsbury, 2021

A catalogue record for this book is available from the British Library.

Library of Congress Cataloging-in-Publication Data
Names: Ambrose, Gavin, author. | Harris, Paul, 1925- author.
Title: Grids for graphic designers / Gavin Ambrose and Paul Harris.
Other titles: Grids
Description: London ; New York : Bloomsbury Visual Arts, 2021. | Series:
Basics design | Previously published: 2012 by AVA Academia under the
title Grids. | Includes bibliographical references and index.
Identifiers: LCCN 2020006988 (print) | LCCN 2020006989 (ebook) | ISBN
9781474254779 (pb) | ISBN 9781474255608 (pdf) | ISBN 9781474255592
(ebook)
Subjects: LCSH: Grids (Typographic design) | Graphic design (Typography)
Classification: LCC Z246 .A553 2021 (print) | LCC Z246 (ebook) | DDC
686.2/2—dc23
LC record available at https://lccn.loc.gov/2020006988
LC ebook record available at https://lccn.loc.gov/2020006989

ISBN: PB: 978-1-474254-77-9
            ePDF: 978-1-474255-60-8
            eBook: 978-1-474255-59-2

Series: Basics Design

Typeset by Lachina Creative, Inc.
Printed and bound in India

To find out more about our authors and books visit
www.bloomsbury.com and sign up for our newsletters.

8–99/01

Client: Reklambyråboke

Design: Gabor Palotai D

Grid properties: A simp
grid creates a strong sen
of identity

RBS 98–99
REKLAMBYRÅER I SVERIGE
ADVERTISING AGENCIES IN SWEDEN

RBS 00/2001
REKLAMBYRÅER I SVERIGE
ADVERTISING AGENCIES IN SWEDEN

/02

BYRÅBOKEN RB2001/02
COMMUNICATION AGENCIES IN SWEDEN

/20

RBS 99/2000
REKLAMBYRÅER I SVERIGE
ADVERTISING AGENCIES IN SWEDEN

eklambyråboken
rochure covers for the national organization of advertising agencies in Swe
he grid forms order and creates a sense of care and craft. This considered
acement of items helps to create an overall identity to the literature

Bedow

Gabor Palotai Design

NB: Studio

3 Deep Design

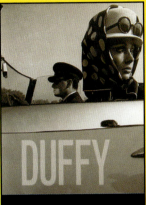

Webb & Webb

Lost & Found Creative

Contents

A grid is the foundation upon which a design is constructed. It allows the designer to effectively organize various elements on a page. In essence, it is the skeletal structure of a piece of work. Grids bring order and structure to designs, whether they are as simple as the one pictured opposite, or as heavily populated as those on newspaper websites.

This book aims to introduce the basic principles of grid usage in graphic design as practised by contemporary designers. Many of these fundamentals date back centuries to when books first started to be mass produced. However, these methods have been refined, improved and complemented throughout the ages. This process continues as new technology brings forth new media, such as Internet pages and mobile telephones.

However, this book is not intended to be a prescriptive guide to setting up and using grids. Instead, we will look at the principles behind grid usage in order to give you the ability to tackle a wide variety of graphic design problems. We believe that a static and repetitive approach to grid use does not result in effective and creative designs. By developing a clear understanding of the many facets of the grid, we hope to prove that grids not only bring order to a design, but also provide ample opportunities for expression and creativity.

Chapter 1: The need for grids

Grids are necessary guides that provide order to the elements of a design, helping readers to access information easily.

Chapter 2: Grid basics

This section is an introduction to the elements that make up a grid, which includes measurements, shapes, proportions and various rules relating to the anatomy of a page.

Chapter 3: Grid types

This chapter shows the relationships between grids, typography and images by exploring and presenting some of the many different grid types available.

Chapter 4: Grid elements

The grid is used to position the various picture, text and graphic elements comprising a design to produce different visual presentations.

Chapter 5: Grid usage

Here, different grids and techniques are discussed to provide a guide for structuring and presenting different types of content including the use of orientation, juxtaposition and space division.

Chapter 6: Online grids

This chapter covers special design considerations for producing grids and layouts for web pages and other electronic media.

.SE (facing page)

Shown here are spreads from a catalogue for .SE – the foundation responsible for the Swedish top-level domain registrations. The grid uses a series of indents and interventions to create a sense of movement, pace and 'typographic colour'.

Client: .SE
Design: Bedow
Grid properties: Indents and mixed column widths creating an expressive grid

Medarbetarnas engagemang och utveckling

Engagemang och delaktighet driver oss framåt. Vi tror att delaktiga och motiverade medarbetare känner större arbetsglädje, är mer engagerade och därmed når ännu bättre resultat. Vi tror också att en gemensam känsla för vad .SE är ger oss större förståelse för vad kunderna vill ha och behöver.

Vår verksamhet bygger till stor del på kunskap och därför är personalen vår viktigaste tillgång. För att alla medarbetare ska kunna växa med företaget och möta den snabba utvecklingen på området vi verkar inom satsar vi på kontinuerlig kompetensutveckling. Samtliga medarbetare har individuella utvecklingsplaner som följs upp varje år.

Genomlyst organisation

Vi är en platt och transparent organisation där det är lätt att identifiera ambitioner och intressen. Medarbetar- och målsamtal är en viktig grund för att fånga upp individernas egna tankar och engagemang. Det finns goda möjligheter att göra karriär för den som har vilja att växa och utvecklas. Den flexibla organisationen gör det möjligt att ge medarbetare möjlighet till mancemang i form av fler befogenheter eller internrekrytering till högre befattningar.

Processtyrd planering

Alla medarbetare är involverade i verksamhetens planering. Affärsplanen tas fram i en process där varje avdelning utarbetar sina egna delmål och handlingsplaner, från de huvudmål och strategier som ledning och styrelse formulerar vid det årliga strategimötet i maj. Därefter bryts affärsplanens strategier, mål och handlingsplaner ner på individnivå.

Under 2009 infördes ett belöningssystem med möjlighet att få upp till en tredjedel av sin lön som bonus.

Korta kommunikationsvägar

Vi har satsat på att få våra medarbetare att må bra och känna sig uppskattade, inte minst genom det förmånspaket som .SE erbjuder sina anställda. Minst lika viktigt är den platta och transparenta organisationen med nära kontakt med närmaste chef, övrig ledning och vd. Dörren till vd står alltid öppen, kan gör på daglig rundor på kontoret och leder måndagsmöten där alla deltar. Förslag till förbättringar uppmuntras och beslutsvägarna är korta. Vi uppmärksammar också när vi når viktiga mål – muntligt på veckomöten, med kaffe och bullar eller tårtkalas och ibland med fest.

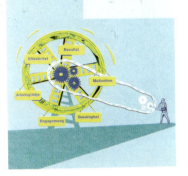

Raketen – verksamhetens processer

Raketen illustrerar hur vi arbetar för att nå våra företagsövergripande, strategiska mål kontinuerlig tillväxt med bibehållen kvalitet och ett starkt samhällsengagemang.

Tillväxt

Vi eftersträvar en kontinuerlig tillväxt för att kunna garantera finansiering av våra satsningar på forskning och utveckling.

Kvalitet

Att vi bibehåller kvalitet gentemot våra kunder, registrarer och medarbetare förmedlar bilden av .SE som det självklara valet.

> *.SE:s verksamhet andas kvalitet, robusthet och säkerhet i alla processer.*

Två typer av ledningsprocesser beslutar om organisationens mål och långsiktiga strategier: Initierande processer som syftar till att hitta nya affärsområden eller produkter och stödjer oss i den långsiktiga planeringen och styrningen samt styrande processer som styr, utvecklar eller samordnar levererande processer och stödprocesser.

.SE:s levererande- eller värdeskapande - processer är utveckling, försäljning, leverans och kundvärd. Dessa realiserar affärsidéen och uppfyller våra externa kunders behov och förväntningar. De bildar tillsammans ett ekosystem som utgör grunden för vår verksamhet. De levererande processerna skapar intäkter och andra värden för .SE och tillbör själva "fabriken". Vi illustrerar dem i ett kretslopp som är föremål för ständig förbättring, där varje del (produkt, projekt) har sitt eget kretslopp.

Våra stödprocesser är resurser som används i de levererande processerna. Dessa är kommunikation, personal, IT-stöd, ekonomi, juridik samt kontorsadministration.

Samhällsengagemang

.SE:s verksamhet andas kvalitet, robusthet och säkerhet i alla processer och bygger på en tydlig affärs- och distributionsmodell. Vi har ständig fokus på förbättringar av både kostnadseffektivitet och kundnytta vilkas bidrar till att vi kan ha en hög nivå på vårt samhällsengagemang. Våra medarbetare är nöjda, kompetenta, känner att de utvecklas och deltar i utvecklingen av Internet i Sverige. Vi ser vårt arbete som del i en större helhet och som att vi aktivt medverkar till förbättringar i samhället.

Raketen leder oss dit vi vill.

Client: ISTD
Design: Grade Design
Grid properties: Expressive
typographic experiment using
house numbers and
postcodes

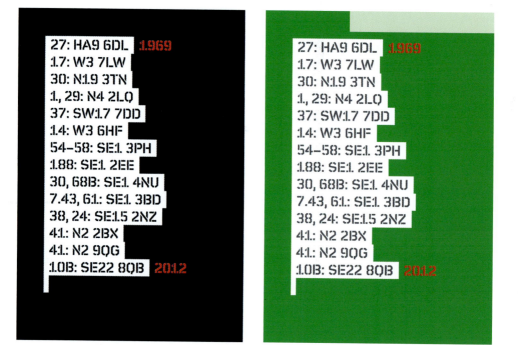

ISTD

Peter Dawson of Grade Design was one of a selection of designers, including the late Alan Fletcher, Derek Birdsall, John Sorrell and Michael Johnson, to participate in an exhibition by the ISTD (International Society of Typographic Designers). The exhibition explored the designers' relationship with London and Peter's poster charts his life in the city through a series of house numbers and postcodes, tracing his movements from college through to work. The typographic forms in turn create a dynamic shape through the irregularity of the line lengths.

Chapter 1
The need for grids

Before looking at grids in detail, this first chapter will look at the basic purpose of a grid and why they are used by graphic designers. Subsequent chapters will look at the placement of elements within a grid and how this impacts the overall design.

A grid provides a structure for all the design elements of a page, which eases and simplifies both the creative and decision-making process for the designer. Using a grid allows for greater accuracy and consistency in the placement of page elements providing a framework for a high degree of creativity. Grids allow a designer to make informed decisions and to use their time efficiently. They can be used to add a high degree of dynamism to a design – the positioning of what may seem a rather small and irrelevant element, such as a folio, can create a dramatic impact on a page, which pulses through a printed work.

Although many of us now view content in an electronic format or via the Web, the structural principles behind the design of a printed page still apply, as the way in which we read a page and extract information from it remains the same.

'A work of art is realized when form and content are indistinguishable.'

Paul Rand

Organizing information

The basic function of a grid is to organize the information on a page. The way in which this is achieved has been developed and refined throughout history.

The grid should be used to aid the placement, order, hierarchy and structure of a design, be it for print, web or environmental application.

Although the grid has developed considerably over time, the basic principles underpinning it have remained intact for centuries. The basic underlining 'rules' have been subject to much study, and the exploration of the grid became of particular interest to Swiss modernists, such as Josef Müller-Brockmann, as shown in his manifesto of the grid.

'The use of the grid implies
- the will to systematize, to clarify
- the will to penetrate to the essentials, to concentrate the will to cultivate objectivity instead of subjectivity
- the will to rationalize the creative and technical production processes
- the will to integrate elements of colour, form and material
- the will to achieve architectural dominion over surface and space
- the will to adopt a positive, forward-thinking attitude
- the recognition of the importance of education and the effect of work devised in a constructive and creative spirit.'

Josef Müller-Brockmann

Fr. Ant. Niedermayr (facing page)

This magazine for a specialist printing company uses a variety of grids to present an engaging narrative. Considering how a product will be used, be it a website or a printed book, is crucial – as well as how people will interact with it. The grid, as in this example, can be seen as a valuable tool that can be used to excite, invigorate and order a design.

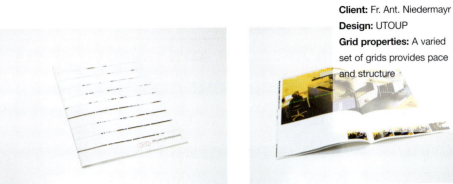

Client: Fr. Ant. Niedermayr
Design: UTOUP
Grid properties: A varied set of grids provides pace and structure

Organizing information

How we read a page

A page will have active and passive areas due to the type of content and the way in which we naturally view a page. It is therefore worth considering how the eye scans a page to locate information.

The active and passive areas of design

A designer has a great deal of freedom in placing different design elements within a layout. However, the way in which the human eye scans an image or a body of text means that certain areas of a page are 'hotter' or more active than others, creating both central and peripheral areas within a page. Designers can use this knowledge to direct the placement of key design elements in order to make them either more prominent or less noticeable.

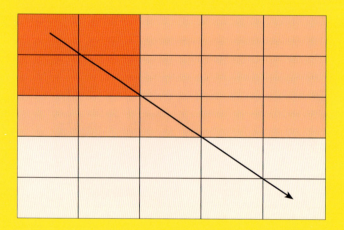

When faced with a new page of information, the human eye habitually looks for an entrance at the top left and scans down and across to the bottom right corner, as shown in the illustration. The depth of colours in this diagram corresponds to the level of the focus of attention being applied (with red being the strongest).

Phaidon (facing page)

These two spreads are from a book about the Arts and Crafts Movement created by Webb & Webb. It features colour images in the principal hotspot at the top, left-hand corner of the page. The use of images excites the eye with a burst of colour and draws the viewer into the spreads. The placement of both text and image elements on the grid adds a subtle movement to the spreads without creating confusion and inhibiting reading. In this instance, the grid 'contains' the elements without stifling them.

Client: Phaidon
Design: Webb & Webb
Grid properties: Colour images in the grid are located in the main hotspot of the spreads

CRAFT AND COMRADESHIP – SOCIAL VISIONS

THOMAS JAMES COBDEN-SANDERSON
Cover of William Morris's *Utopia* (1890, fig. 57)

IN THE 1860s AND 1870s THE ARTS AND CRAFTS HAD BEEN CHARACTERIZED BY AN INTERLACING WEB OF THEMES. IN THE 1880s AND 1890s, HOWEVER, ONE STRAND CAME TO THE FORE – THAT OF FELLOWSHIP.

This was linked to the rise of socialism, with its agenda of shifting systems of power and means of production from private hands to the community as a whole. Many members of the Arts and Crafts Movement in Britain became committed socialists, its byword of social inclusion matching their concern to democratize the arts. Fellowship as a form of empowerment also developed in other walks of life, from welfare and science to education and philanthropy, and while some of the groups which resulted were little more than clubs for hard drinking and gluttonous dining, others, such as the Institution of Civil Engineers, were committed to a specific cause. There was a rise in the membership of Friendly Societies, a network of working-class clubs which stemmed from trade-related associations of the eighteenth century, and offered subsidies such as sickness and funeral benefits (by 1880, membership had reached approximately 2 million). From the middle of the century trade unionism was also on the increase, and in 1884 the Fabian Society was established with the aim of engaging in non-revolutionary reform along socialist lines. On a less political level, there was everything from the literary and philosophical societies, which increased rapidly from the 1820s, to the intriguing Society for the Suppression of Vice.

Whatever their size or purpose, their groups all shared a fundamental sense of community. This had featured strongly in the rhetoric of Pugin, Ruskin and Morris, and in the 1880s was to become a defining characteristic of the British Arts and Crafts Movement. As Morris insisted in his socialist story, *A Dream of John Ball*, which was published in instalments from 1886 to 1887: 'Fellowship is heaven, and lack of fellowship is hell; fellowship is life, and lack of fellowship is death.' Reflecting this sentiment, a succession of craft guilds, workshops and societies began to develop throughout Britain, in city centres and rural retreats, with formal manifestos or simple bonds of friendship each realizing to varying degrees the social, creative and, on occasion, philanthropic aims of the Arts and Crafts. If, up until now, the Movement had been a set of ideas and aspirations shared by a few assertive and charismatic individuals, in the 1880s it acquired a wide support base, a coherent identity and, in 1887, a name, when the writer and bookbinder Thomas James Cobden-Sanderson (1840–1922) coined the phrase The Arts and Crafts.

Some of the earliest craft associations of the period were run by women, for whom the applied arts had long been an acceptable form of activity. In 1872 Elizabeth Wardle,

53

How we read a page

Client: Paris 2012
Olympic Committee
Design: Research Studios
Grid properties: Colour
hotspots are used to
draw attention

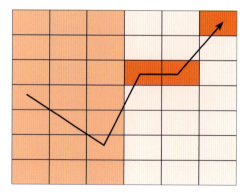

This illustration depicts the hotspots of the spread above. Notice how the title and folio have more pull than the image.

Paris 2012 Olympic Committee

This brochure was created by Research Studios for the 2012 Olympic architectural bids. It features the use of colour to create visual hotspots. While the full-bleed image may initially draw attention, the red titling and indicator mark grab the reader's attention as the eye naturally scans to the right and is then pulled to the text, as shown on the left. Notice how the text is roughly aligned to the form of the subject of the image, the Arc de Triomphe in Paris.

Client: The Waterways Trust
Design: Pentagram
Grid properties: A text entry point is created through colour contrast

Our Involvement
The Caledonian Canal

The Caledonian Canal runs through the Great Glen, one of the world's most spectacular and picturesque routes, from Inverness through Loch Ness, Loch Oich and Loch Lochy to Fort William. A programme of restoration of the locks is being led by British Waterways and will secure navigation along its entire length for the future.

Over the next three years, The Waterways Trust Scotland will support the programme assisting with funding for the heritage landscape elements of the restoration. Subject to a feasibility study, The Trust plans to restore Scot II, a unique icebreaker built especially for the Canal in the early part of the 20th century. The plan includes an on-board environmental education facility which The Trust will develop with other partners.

Top left
Evening on the Caledonian Canal.

Top centre
The Canal at Fort Augustus.

Top right
Views of the Highlands from the Canal.

Right
Yachts are regular users of the Caledonian Canal.

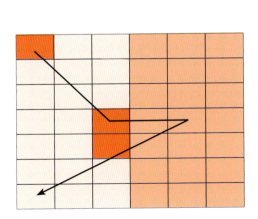

This illustration shows that the white text sections reversed out of the blue verso page represent the main hotspots on the spread above.

The Waterways Trust

Pentagram's brochure for The Waterways Trust uses white text against a dark background to form hotspots that serve as entry points for the eye, which mirrors the effect on the opposite page.

The page has a clear sense of 'flow' enforced by the grid structure – there is a clear pattern of movement from title, to image, to text and finally to caption.

How we read a page

How we view a screen

People scan web pages in the same way that they scan a printed page – that is, to search for key words or things of interest. A designer can aid this process by introducing visual 'entry points', or by creating a simple hierarchy of information.

F-pattern for reading web content

Research has shown that people tend to read web pages in an F-shaped pattern. They quickly scan across the top from left to right in two stripes, and then scan down the page as they rapidly move forward in search of something meaningful. In terms of design, this means that key information and entry points should be located within the ambit of the F-pattern to increase the chances of catching (and holding) the reader's attention.

The fold

With web pages, you also need to consider the fold. This is the area of a site that has to be scrolled to be visible. The fold of a web page is the imaginary line that limits what you can see before having to scroll down. The smaller the screen or the lower the screen resolution, the higher up the content fold will occur. Key information should be located above the fold to minimize the amount of searching that viewers will have to do. It is also worth remembering that if the design relies on scrolling down beyond the 'fold' point, not all viewers will see the secondary content. For this reason, it is important that the design structure effectively uses and maximizes the impact of the top portion of the grid.

Dan Tobin Smith (facing and following pages)

Photographer Dan Tobin Smith's website, designed by Studio Output, uses simple and effective navigation, as all the information is laid out and compatible with the F-shaped reading pattern. The featured photographic works, displayed as thumbnails on a grid, can be enlarged to fill the screen. While a visible and dominant element, the grid still enables enjoyment of the imagery shown on the site; the pattern formed by the grid adds a further layer of tension and interest.

DAN TOBIN SMITH
STILL LIFE
INTERIORS/INSTALLATION
ADVERTISING
SERIES
SHOWREEL
ARCHIVE
CONTACT

Client: Dan Tobin Smith
Design: Studio Output
Grid properties: Simple navigation compatible with the F-shaped scanning motion

How we view a screen

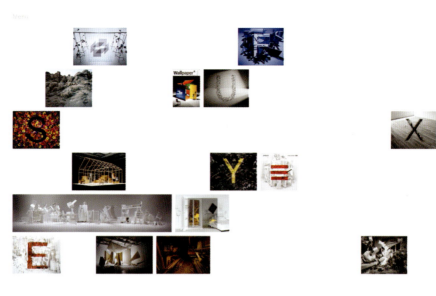

Back to Interiors/Installation

How we view a screen

Form and function

While a designer should take into account the physical limitations and requirements of the media or format being used, the form of a design should (arguably) be subsidiary to its function. A project's form will vary according to the target audience that it is being designed for.

The modernist standpoint that 'form follows function' can be useful during the initial design stages when starting to think about a piece of communication. To a certain extent, a grid's form will be dictated by its function. Who is it aimed at? How will it be used? Where will it be read? By asking a series of questions, the design will often manifest itself. For example, a grid that is appropriate for a cookery book will have specific requirements and will not also necessarily accommodate an annual report, sales catalogue or newspaper listing. A useful guiding principle for effective design is that a design should be easy to use and readily accessible to its intended audience. Not all design is functional, however, and the grid can and should also be used in expressive and experimental ways.

Modernism

'Form follows function' is a phrase attributed to the architect Louis Sullivan. It succinctly captures the notion that the demands of practical use be placed above aesthetic considerations in design. This ideological approach proposed doing away with superfluous adornment in order to focus principally on usability.

ISTD (facing and following pages)

This issue of *TypoGraphic, the Journal of the International Society of Typographic Designers*, took as its theme the notion of contrast, which reflects the varied nature of the journal. Contributions were supplied by Jack Stauffacher, Mikhail Karasik and Sebastian Carter. The bold colour scheme and presentation of information in blocks is used to reinforce the theme.

Client: ISTD
Design: Peter Dawson and Tegan Danko, Grade Design
Grid properties: A grid inspired by the theme of the journal – 'contrast'

Contrast n.
a difference which is clearly seen when two things are compared.

ISTD TypoGraphic 66 The Contrast Issue

Form and function

Meeting
Jack Stauffacher

Michael Harvey

Photo: Dennis Letbetter

Every weekday morning, the ferry from Tiburon and Sausalito carries dark-suited young executives grasping black document cases headed for San Francisco's financial district, and a tanned older man with abundant white hair, wearing a light suit accompanied by a vintage Italian racing bicycle. Arriving at the Ferry Building on Fishermans' Wharf, he crosses the Embarcadero, mounts his bike and rides up the hill along Broadway to number 300, a one-time printers' building, takes the elevator to the third floor and enters the office of The Greenwood Press, an imprint he established over seventy years ago. The cyclist is Jack Werner Stauffacher, printer, scholar, author, typographer, designer, and in his youth a skilled bicycle polo player. Now in his eighty-sixth year he is the most youthful and most invigorating man I know.

Stauffacher was born in San Francisco in 1920, and his family moved to San Mateo shortly afterwards in 1922. In 1934 he purchased a 3 x 5 inch Kelsey Press, and two years later built a studio in the family back garden, acquiring a Chandler & Price 10 x 15 platen press and a large selection of Garamond fonts from American Type Foundry. Here, under The Greenwood Press imprint he printed business cards and tickets. Before long he had visited several of San Francisco's printing masters: Nash, the Grabhorns, Taylor & Taylor. Six years later he published his first book, *Three Choice Sketches by Geoffrey Crayon, Gent* by Washington Irving, the whole book handset 'under the open sky of San Mateo'.

That year his brother Frank made a short film about bicycle polo, and the following year Jack published *Bicycle Polo: Technique and Fundamentals*.

Drafted into the army in 1942 he shut the press, re-opening it two years later on his discharge. Connections with the literary scene in the Bay Area led to printing two issues of *Circle* magazine, and he cycled to Monterey and Big Sur where he met Henry Miller and Jean Varda. In 1945 he printed his first book after the war, *Henry Miller Miscellanea*. Knowing that Miller was a keen cyclist Jack bought him a machine and shipped it to Big Sur.

His brother Frank's film work led to the designing and printing of *Art in Cinema*, a catalogue for the Art in Cinema Society which became a rallying point for young film enthusiasts, and a visit to Los Angeles to meet Man Ray and Luis Buñuel. Type was also a consuming interest, Updike's *Printing Types* was a touchstone, and the traditional forms of Baskerville and Garamond were respected for their clarity. The works of Goethe illuminated Jack's growing understanding of the past and present of art.

The press moved from San Mateo to San Francisco, and in 1947 Jack collaborated with the distinguished typographer, scholar and writer Adrian Wilson, working together at the press to publish Eric Gill's *And Who Wants Peace?* Gill's typographical canon, his type designs shaped by hand and eye, appealed to both men. *Fifteen Letters* from Switzerland,

A simple grid is punctuated by colour tints overlaying photography, lending a sense of depth and texture to the pages.

Hierarchy is added using varying typographic sizes and colours, with a single weight, which operate within a rigid set of constraints. The resulting spreads and grids are distinctly contemporary, whilst paying homage to the modernist approach.

Form and function

Client: Antique Collectors Club
Design: Webb & Webb
Grid properties: Simple grid prioritizing image presentation

A grid has been used loosely for the spreads pictured here, in order to give prominence to the images.

Antique Collectors Club

These spreads are from a publication that uses a simple grid to give priority to the images. The form of the grid is dictated by its function: to focus on the images and give them sufficient space. The top spread features works by Edward Bawden and Eric Ravilious; the spread below has works by Paul Nash and John Nash.

Client: Luke Hughes & Company
Design: Webb & Webb
Grid properties: Dynamic folio placement, and strong sense of product placement

St Swithin's

Luke Hughes & Company

This book on bespoke chairs was designed for Luke Hughes & Company. It features the dynamic placement of folios within red circles, which are positioned on the outside edge of the pages. The central alignment of the red circles effectively draws attention, and their appearance on the recto pages prompts the reader to turn the page.

Form and function

Images dominate these spreads and the bold placement of the folio (top) brings a sense of movement to the design. The grid is explicitly used (bottom) by showing a collage of details that draw attention to the quality of the company's product.

Client: Salon Haagse
Design:
Faydherbe/De Vringer
Grid properties: Central axis and active perimeter underpin strong composition

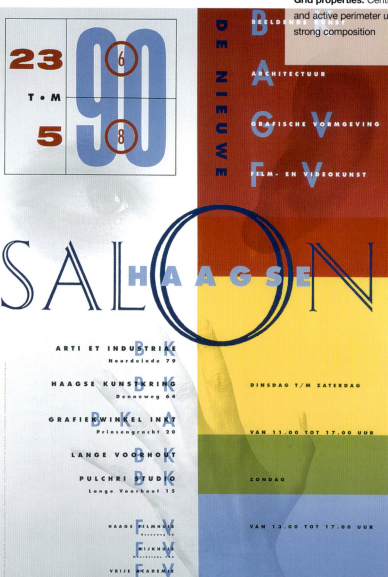

Chapter 2
Grid basics

A grid is the basic framework within which a design is created. It provides a reference structure that guides the placement of the elements forming the anatomy of a design, such as text, images and illustrations, in addition to general elements such as straplines and folios.

As a grid delineates the space on a page or spread, effective grid use requires a good understanding of the absolute and relative measurements used to form it. The grid is not a prescriptive design tool, however, and there are various ways of using grids in order to produce a dynamic design. This may include the creation of active hotspots or shapes; the use of different proportions to add movement; or establishing a hierarchy.

'Admit constraints: then, having admitted, fill with discovery.'

Anthony Froshaug

Grid basics

Salon Haagse (facing page)

This Salon Haagse poster created by Faydherbe/De Vringer has page elements that align to a central axis, which produces a visually strong composition. The text at the top and bottom creates an active perimeter within a balanced and graphically strong composition, while the mix of typefaces, type sizes, alignments and colours creates a clear and easy-to-navigate hierarchy.

Anatomy of a page
A page is made up of several distinct parts and each section has a significant purpose and function in the overall design.

Fore-edge/outer margin
The outer margin that helps frame the presentation of text within a design.

Gutter
The margin area that occurs in the fold between two pages of a spread. Also the space between two text columns.

Image modules
Spaces created within a grid for the placement of pictorial elements.

Baseline grid
The basic structure used to guide the placement of text and other elements within a design.

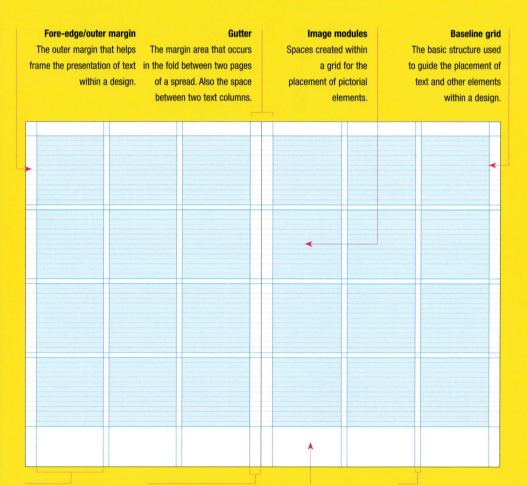

Column
Spaces for the organized presentation of body text that help to make the text readable. This layout features six text columns over the two-page spread.

Back edge/inner margin
The margin that is closest to the spine or centre fold, which is also called a 'gutter'.

Foot/bottom margin
The margin found at the bottom of the page.

Intercolumn space
The space separating two columns, which is also called a 'gutter'.

Client: Park House

Design: Third Eye Design

Grid properties: Text column is used as a visual element, adding colour to the overall design

The legendary West End. In parks and museums, circuses and crescents, there's space to wander, places to think. Pop into cosy cafes and corner delis. Window shop in eclectic stores and sip something chilled in a cool bar (or something cool in a chilled bar). In cobbled lanes and leafy greens, you walk the walk of history. Fine architecture and notable Scots: writers, scientists, musicians and politicians.

The City. All day and all night. The crowds hustle. The bustle. And the banter. An ear to the bright lights. The city sights. A haven (a heaven) for shoppers and clubbers; bon and pub regulars.

A world of possibility in a few square miles. Visit beautiful art galleries and museums. over that must-have outfit. Catch the chai a latte and savour every last mouthful of th chef's special.

The Legendary West End

Bright Lights City Sights

Anatomy of a page

Park House

Each design involves making many decisions about the placement of its different elements. The use of a grid allows a designer to make decisions in a controlled and coherent manner, instead of relying on judgement alone. Third Eye Design's spreads for Park House incorporate many design facets, such as the placement of type, folios, titles and images. Notice how the text column is treated as a visual element, adding a block of colour to the design. This is obtained by implementing strategic placement using the image modules and uniform column spacing.

Grids can be used to present multiple images in ways that help to build the narrative of a publication. The example featured uses juxtapositions and different sizes on the recto page, which impose a hierarchy according to importance. The images create a narrative that leads the eye across the spread.

Measurements
There are two types of measurements used in graphic design: absolute and relative measurements.

The grid itself is typically constructed with absolute measurements, such as inches or points, while many of the items that are placed within it may use relative measurements, meaning that their size and position are determined in relation to the grid.

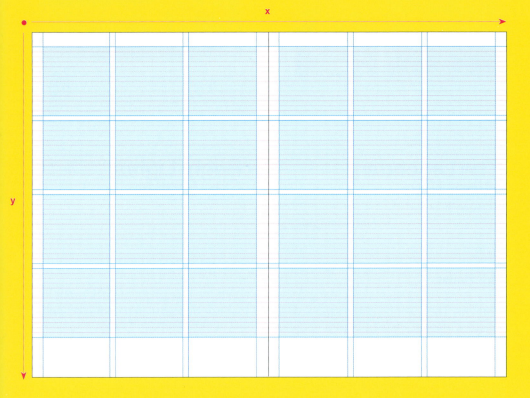

When working with grids, it is possible to use coordinates taken from a starting point, such as the top left-hand corner in this example. The magenta lines represent a baseline grid that is set at 12pt intervals, with the first line and column representing coordinates (1,1). The image fields are a relative measurement of 14 lines of the baseline grid, which at 12pts apart gives 168pt square image units (14x12). Intercolumn spaces or gutters are set at 12pts, with fore and outer margins set at 24pts, and the head margin at 36pts.

Type

Type is usually determined in points, which is an absolute measurement. As absolute measurements give a fixed value for determined lengths, it means that both type and the baseline grid it sits upon have a spatial compatibility. It is possible to work with type in points and the baseline in millimetres, but it is easier if both elements share the same measurement system.

Images

Digital images are normally placed into a design as a percentage relative to their full size, or resized to fit a specific space. However, in order to reproduce well in print, an image needs to have a resolution of at least 300ppi (an image needs to be 72ppi for on-screen usage).

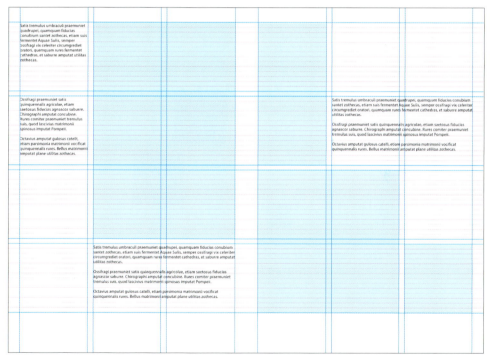

Blocks of type typically have a relative measurement – they may occupy a column, a portion of a column, or straddle several columns, such as the two-column blocks above. In this instance, once a grid is established, absolute measurements become of secondary importance.

An image can also occupy a single module or cover a series of modules, as represented by the blue boxes in the example above.

Measurements

Shapes on a page
The composition of a design is constructed of type and image elements, which essentially form shapes on a page.

The grid has strong links to certain artistic movements such as cubism, constructivism and other branches of modernism, which give preference to a strict use of structure.

Text and image elements can be treated as shapes in order to produce a coherent and effective design. Designers can draw the viewer's attention in a similar way to a painter composing elements on a canvas. The different shapes capture the eye and form a series of relationships, which add to the message of the design or painting. The following pages provide a synopsis of some common design compositions.

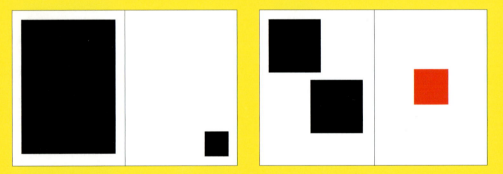

The illustrations above introduce the idea of placing elements on a page to create visual shapes. Objects can dominate a page or simply sit as a shy insertion in the corner; they can establish relationships with one another or clearly be different to everything else.

Thames & Hudson (facing page)

In this book, *The Snow Show*, Grade Design make explicit use of shapes on a page. This breaking of pattern and grid adds interest and encourages the reader to turn the page. The balance between creating continuity and adding interest is what makes this such a successful design – it is simultaneously calm and dynamic.

Client: Thames & Hudson
Design: Grade Design
Grid properties: Pace and movement added through the use of distinct shapes on the page

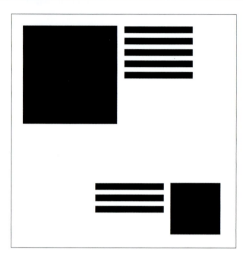

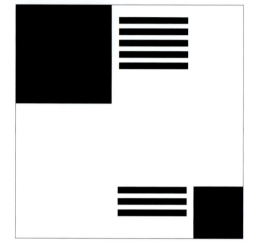

Grouping

Elements are grouped to form units or blocks of related information. Aligning the edges of the different design elements helps to establish connections between them. The grouping method works by separating blocks into distinct zones on the page, spread or even publication.

Perimeter

Elements are grouped to make dramatic use of the page's perimeter with images bleeding off. The perimeter is often avoided in a design to maintain a neat frame or passepartout. However, it can also be used creatively and effectively to add drama and movement to a piece.

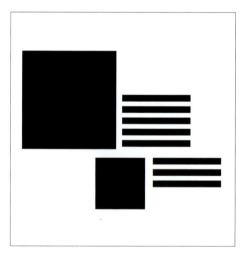

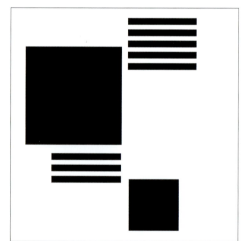

Horizontal

Page elements have a horizontal emphasis that draws the eye of the viewer across the page. This is further examined on page 78.

Vertical

Page elements have a vertical stress that leads the eye of the viewer up and down the page. This technique is further discussed on page 80.

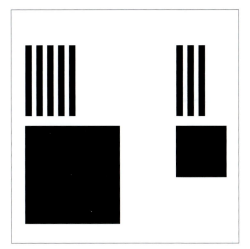

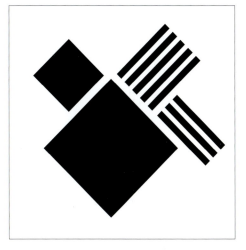

Broadside

Text is presented so that it reads vertically rather than horizontally, forcing the viewer to adjust their physical relation to the page. This method is often used to present tabular material that is too long for a standard page, further discussed on page 84.

Angular

Angular text also forces the viewer to change their relationship to the page. Although type and images can be set at any angle, it is good practice to use a unified setting for consistency, such as the 45-degree angle used in the example above. This type of orientation is further examined on page 86.

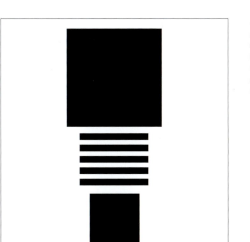

Axis orientated

The page elements are consciously set to align to an axis, such as the vertical centre pictured here. However, alignment can be in any direction. This orientation is looked at in more detail on page 140.

Passepartout

This is a common way of presenting photos whereby the image dominates the space on the page and is marked by a border.

Shapes on a page

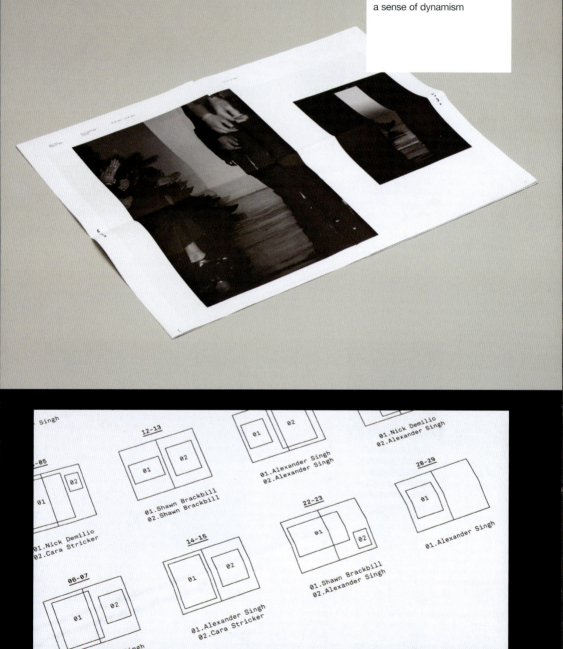

Client: Alex Singh
Design: Ömse
Grid properties: Variations in scale and placement create a sense of dynamism

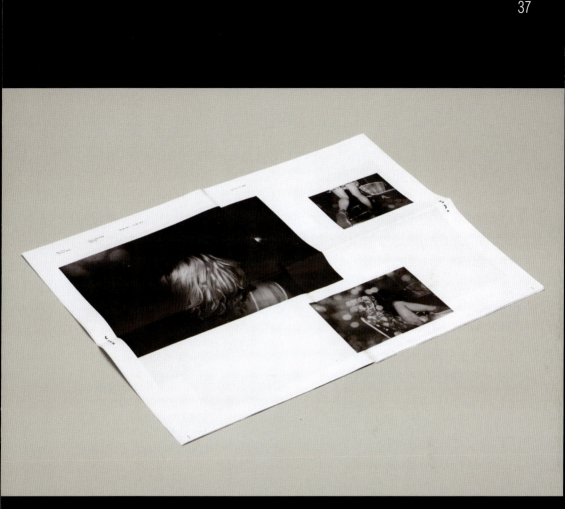

Void Paper

James Kape and Briton Smith, who collaborate as Ömse, designed this
newspaper featuring images of New York Fashion Week by photographers
Alex Singh, Shawn Brackbill, Nick D'Emilio and Cara Stricker. Variety in
position and size creates a sense of pace and dynamic movement.

Shapes on a page

Industry view:
Lavernia & Cienfuegos Diseño

Lavernia & Cienfuegos Diseño is a design practice based in Valencia, Spain. Founded by Nacho Lavernia and Alberto Cienfuegos, the studio works across graphic, industrial and packaging projects. Shown on this and the following page is a publication for renowned architects Fran Silvestre and Alfaro Hofmann.

The book is aimed at the general public, who don't necessarily understand the subtleties of Fran Silvestre and Alfaro Hofmann's work. The design aims to reflect the architects' work – can you expand on how this is achieved?

One of the goals of the architects was that readers could easily understand each project, even if they were not used to looking at architectural photography and could not read a plan correctly. It is not easy to transmit the complexity of a three-dimensional space through the two dimensions of paper, let alone the beauty and visual interest of a space that surrounds you that you are seeing and experiencing from within.

There was a strict process for taking pictures, which also governed their subsequent selection. Often the images in the book explain each other and so they work together as collections of photos that describe the space and the project really well. Occasionally, the beauty of photography simply does do justice to the beauty of real space and manages to provoke a similar aesthetic response in the viewer.

Can you explain how the grid is used to add a sense of harmony and pace to the designs?
For the most important projects included in the book, there is usually a key image – the most representative and spectacular of the project – which is panoramic. This horizontal aspect provides a structure to the book format and internal contents in three distinct ways, as follows:
1. The double page represents the composition space for us. We have never considered the individual page when composing our layouts. Our working unit is the double page.
2. The entire composition is built on a central horizontal axis, which runs from the left fore-edge to the right fore-edge. Images and text blocks are centre-aligned along the vertical plane.

3. The image sizes vary according to their importance and also in terms of their function within the composition. There are no vertical guides. The pictures sometimes exceed the spine edge. What matters is the interplay between the photography and the white space, which sets the rhythm throughout each chapter. This relationship between occupied and empty space, between figure and ground, between mark and frame, is what produces tension, energy or a sense of calm within a publication.

Shown above are the cover and spreads from Arquitectura de la Casa – a publication about the architectural and interior design projects of Fran Silvestre and Alfaro Hofmann. The spreads use a range of image placements to bring harmony, pace and a sense of order to the content, aptly reflecting the architectural concerns of the subject matter. The varying placement of items in relation to the perimeter and gutter of the publication create a playful, delicate sense of pace.

Industry view: Lavernia & Cienfuegos Diseño

Proportion
Proportion is used to create a dynamic between the different elements within a design.

Page dynamics

Changing the proportion of images or text elements within a design can dramatically alter the dynamic of a page. Maintaining the proportions between different elements can be used to show different views of the same item by creating a neutral space. This then allows for passive juxtaposition – where contrasts between elements are presented in their actual differences rather than their proportions. On the other hand, an active juxtaposition is created by changing the proportions of the images, as shown below. The proportion of the images in relation to the size of the page also affects the design's dynamic.

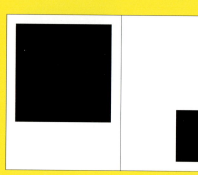

Passive

This illustration features a passive juxtaposition, where the images are presented at the same size. In this case, any differences in the images would create the dynamic.

Active

This illustration features an active juxtaposition, created by altering the proportion of the images. The larger image draws more attention and dominates the spread, giving it more importance.

Gattegno (facing page)

This brochure for dairy producer Gattegno makes use of altering proportions and alignments to create a dynamic and active presentation. This change of placement adds pace and interest to the publication.

Client: Gattegno
Design: Mousegraphics
Grid properties: Dynamics added through the use of proportion and pace

HISTORY

ΙΣΤΟΡΙΑ

DANIEL S. GATTEGNO & SON S.A. was established almost a century ago in Thessaloniki and initially engaged in sugar & coffee trading. After the 2nd World War the company relocated in Athens where it operated in the trade of milk & cocoa, selling its products mainly to the industrial sector.

As the company grows it expands its product portfolio adding consumer products like condensed milk & skimmed milk powder (Regilait). It also enters the cheese market importing Reguto from Northern Ireland & a variety of other cheeses like Gouda, Edam, etc. from West European countries, mainly Germany.

After 1968, taking advantage of the rapid growth of the domestic retail market the company proceeded in the development & trade of private label products.

Today, the company continues importing & selling dairy products, milk & cheese co-operating with all industries of this sector and activating in retail trade. It is also expanding its business in neighbouring Balkan countries.

INDUSTRIAL PRODUCTS

BULK MATERIALS IN TANKS
Fresh raw milk
Fresh pasteurized milk
Fresh skimmed milk pasteurized
Skimmed milk concentrate (LH-HH-HN)
Full cream milk concentrate
Milk cream pasteurized
Sweet or acid whey concentrate
Fresh sheep's milk
Fresh sheep's milk cream
Sweet whey sheep milk concentrate
Fresh goat's milk
Fresh goat milk concentrate

BULK MATERIALS IN BAGS
Sweet or acid whey in powder
Skimmed milk powder (LH-HH-HN)
Full cream milk powder (LH-HH-HN)
Butter
Butter oil
Frozen sheep's or goat's cream
Sheep's frozen white cheese crumbles

PRODUCT CATEGORIES
a. consumer dairy goods
b. industrial dairy products & materials
c. private label products

ΚΑΤΗΓΟΡΙΕΣ ΠΡΟΙΟΝΤΩΝ
α. καταναλωτικά προϊόντα γαλακτοκομικά
β. βιομηχανικά γαλακτοκομικά προϊόντα & ύλες
γ. προϊόντα ιδιωτικής ετικέτας

CONSUMER PRODUCTS

SUSTAINABLE ADVANTAGE (U.S.P)
Our long history & exceptional knowledge of the European dairy industry allows us to offer our clients the desired differentiation & unique developmental opportunities, resulting to optimal market penetration for quicker & better aimed growth.

Proportion

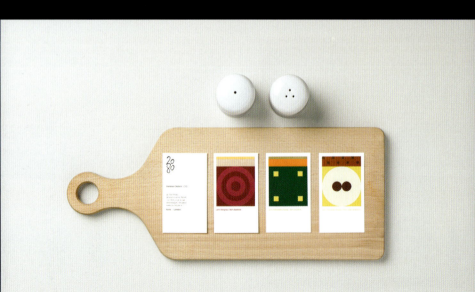

20/80

20/80 was a new brand entering the crowded food sector and in particular, the short attention span 'food-to-go' market.

The client's aim was to create a healthy but easily understandable, simplified food offering. This was in direct response to the saturation of messages consumers are confronted with: organic, low fat, reduced sodium and gluten free to name but a few.

The brand is a take on the famous 80/20 rule for dieting, and uses this simple mathematical formula to directly inform the design and structure of the packaging and marketing materials.

80% of the product consists of vegetables or fruits (represented by squares) with the remaining 20% consisting of protein as a garnish (represented by squares, triangles and other graphic elements).

The resulting print materials and graphic identity, with its harmonious proportions and strong graphic identity, helps to create a clear proposition for the brand.

Client: 20/80
Design: Landor
Grid properties: Product informing design proportions

Proportion

Industry view: Gabor Palotai Design

The following case study shows the identity and development work for Riksutställningar, the Swedish Exhibition Agency, undertaken by Gabor Palotai Design.

The work that you have created for the Swedish Exhibition Agency uses a series of typographic characters and basic shapes combined with flat, primary colours. A controlled and ordered grid is also evident. Can you elaborate on how this has developed over the past six years of design work?

Consequence is, of course, of the utmost importance when designing the foundation for a graphic profile. Once the grid system is designed, in tandem with the vision of the design, one can easily create new versions and variables of the graphic profile. The most important thing is to always stick to the concept.

How do you see the idea of a grid fitting with your work?

Everyday life already involves living in a world of grid systems. The grid of my flat. The grid of my space in my studio. The grid of the streets that I walk to get there. And the grid systems in my work.

We need all of these grids. But the most important thing is to know when you need to break all of these rules with humour and play.

Shown opposite are spreads from Riksutställningar's annual report that utilizes a two-column, dual-language grid.

Gabor Palotai Design is a small design studio based in Stockholm, Sweden. They work on a broad range of design projects in the field of visual communication, often making effective use of simple shapes to create engaging and effective designs.
www.gaborpalotai.com

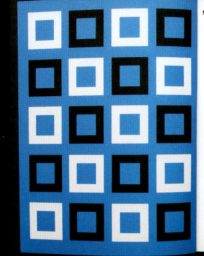

Although these designs are controlled and 'gridded', they have an expressive, playful nature. Is the sense of play and humour important to your design practice?
Humour can be used to make a serious graphic design so much more enchanting.

Can you elaborate on how you see this type of pictogram work fitting into the wider history of graphic design? Are there specific reference points that you are influenced or inspired by?
Egyptian hieroglyphics inspired me. The Phila Temple in Aswan is covered in fantastic pictograms. The experimental geist of the pre-modernists, from the dadaists to the typographers of the russian revolution, who designed art as images, I find lovely because of their straightforwardness and temper. The surrealists make me feel at home, actually. The yellow poster, 'Ceci n'est pas une pipe', is an allegory of Magritte's infamous painting which goes by this title.

Shown here are various posters using simple typographic characters that create an eclectic set of designs.

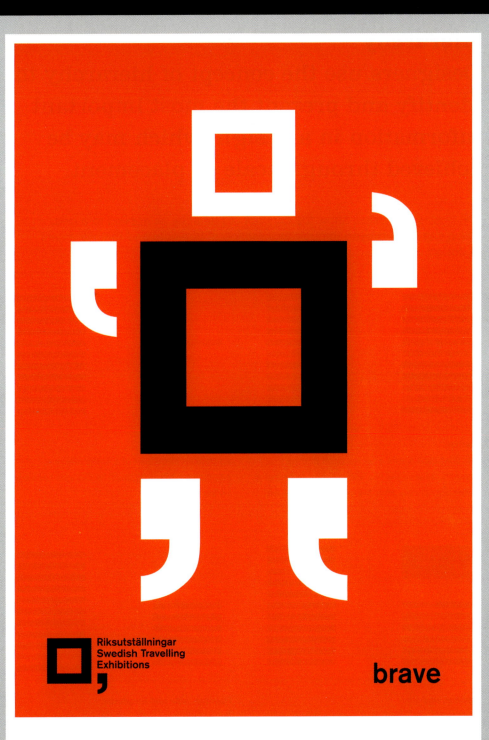

Riksutställningar
Swedish Travelling
Exhibitions

brave

Industry view: Gabor Palotai Design

Hierarchy

Designers use the concept of hierarchy to identify and present the most important information in a design, which may be achieved through scale or placement.

The illustrations below show the concept of hierarchy as applied to a grid, which can be conveyed through the creation of hotspots and the placement of design elements.

Neutral
This illustration shows a neutral page with no hierarchy between the two text columns. Note that a reader will naturally enter the design at the top left.

Position
An obvious placement of a design element introduces a hierarchy, such as this lone heading on the verso page.

Position and size
Positioning an element in the entry hotspot, while also altering its size and introducing spacing, establishes its dominance in the hierarchy.

Position, size and emphasis
A final technique is to add extra emphasis to an element to cement its position at the top of the hierarchy – as seen in the use of colour above.

Client: Black Dog Publishing
Design: Research Studios
Grid properties: Hierarchy is established via folio placement and gutter-crossing large type

Chapter 03

The magazine cover, fashion and photography

Is the fashion magazine cover just body fascism with elegant typography or a mass-market vehicle for women's solidarity and sense of themselves? Photography's ambiguous relationship with 'reality' has enabled it to celebrate the female face and sell clothes, often on the front of the same magazine.

Black Dog Publishing

This book was designed by Research Studios for Black Dog Publishing and it features a hierarchy established by large-scale type. The use of large, centrally placed folios and type crossing the central gutter of some spreads provides a strong sense of movement, leading from one spread to the next. The spreads also convey a sense of 'depth' by layering type and image, and forming combined units of information.

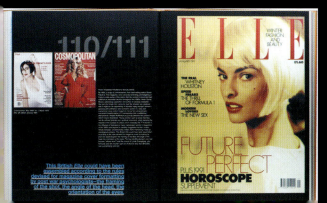

110/111

COSMOPOLITAN

ELLE
WINTER FASHION AND BEAUTY
JANUARY 1991
£1.60

THE REAL WHITNEY HOUSTON

SPEED FREAKS THE THRILL OF FORMULA 1

MODERN LOVERS THE NEW SEX

FUTURE PERFECT

PLUS 1991 HOROSCOPE SUPPLEMENT

This British *Elle* could have been assembled according to the rules devised for magazine cover formatting by post-war psychologists—the framing of the shot, the angle of the head, the orientation of the eyes.

Client: Moxham
Design: Design by Journal
Grid Properties: Simple hierarchy

be established using placement, size and colour. Limiting the number of variables can help to keep the hierarchy both simple enough to use and clear enough to navigate. In this example by Design by Journal, for a look-book by jewellery designer Moxham, a series of design considerations have been made. The images are set using wide and varied passepartouts, or white borders creating a canvas for the typography to be placed over. The typographic styles are limited to three main variables with graphic interventions including generous indentations and underlined headlines which all help to create a sense of order and hierarchy.

Irish Architecture Foundation (opposite)

In this promotional poster for the Irish Architecture Foundation, a single colour is used for all typography, instilling a sense of identity. The typography, based on old cinema signage, is playful but still retains a clear sense of order and hierarchy.

Client: Irish Architecture Foundation
Design: Unthink
Grid properties: Clear hierarchy using a variety of type sizes

Rem Koolhaas
Frank Lloyd Wright
Jem Cohen
Sanaa
Patrick Keiller
Thom Andersen
Wim Wenders
Archigram
Robin Walker
Tilda Swinton
Cedric Price
Ernö Goldfinger
Seamus Heaney
Saskia Sassen
Jacque Tati
The Fourth Wall Symposium
Irish Film Archive

The Irish Architecture Foundation in partnership with the Irish Film Institute presents—

05—15 MAY 2011
IFI DUBLIN

A season on film and architecture illuminating the point of encounter between architecture and the moving image.

Curated by Nathalie Weadick, Director Irish Architecture Foundation and Samantha Martin McAuliffe, UCD School of Architecture. Delivered by GradCam and UCD in partnership with IAF and IFI

Programme details and bookings
www.architecturefoundation.ie
www.ifi.ie

THE FOURTH WALL

Hierarchy

Drawing a grid
Grids can be drawn in a range of ways using different mathematical principles.

Using the proportion of the page
A page size or grid can be created using proportional relationships, such as the one shown in the illustration below. The different elements are a product of the page dimensions.

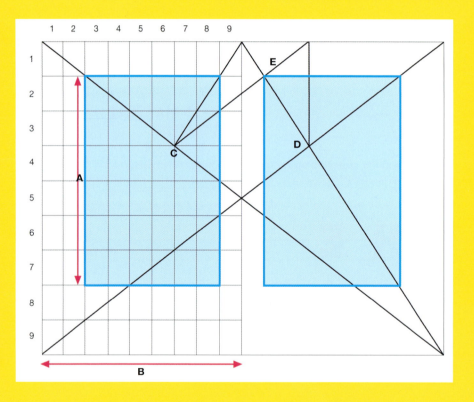

The illustration above represents the classic layout created by typographer Jan Tschichold based on a page with proportions of 2:3. The height of the text block (A) is the same as the width of the page (B), while the spine and head margins are positioned at one-ninth of the page, and the inner margin is half the outer margin. An imaginary, horizontal dissecting line a third of the way down the page intersects the diagonal lines dividing the spread (C) and the recto page (D). A vertical line drawn from (D) to the upper margin is then connected to (C). Where this line intersects the recto page diagonal is the location point for the corner of the text box (E). The text box that results is six units wide and six deep.

Using units

The Fibonacci number series can also be used to obtain proportions for dividing a page as it reflects the harmonious proportions of the 8:13 golden ratio. In the Fibonacci sequence, each number is the sum of the preceding two numbers, and this can be used to determine the values of different units on a page, as shown below.

0, 1, 1, 2, 3, 5, 8, 13, 21, 34, 55, 89, 144...

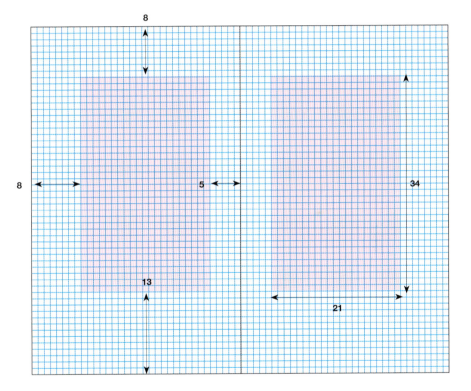

The 34x55 unit grid illustrated above has a text block positioned five units from the inner margin.

The next number in the Fibonacci sequence is eight, which is used to determine the top and outer margins of the text block. The next number is 13 and is used for the bottom margin. Determining the values of the text block in this way creates a coherent and integrated relationship between the width and height. Note that the block is 21x34 units – numbers from the Fibonacci sequence.

Fibonacci sequence

A numerical series where each number is the sum of the preceding two numbers in the sequence. The sequence is named after the mathematician Fibonacci, formally known as Leonardo of Pisa. Fibonacci noted the existence of the sequence in the proportions of the natural world.

Drawing a grid

Developing the grid

The grid below is based on a design by Karl Gerstner for *Capital* magazine. It is a flexible modular grid that maintains column divisions, while allowing different grid structures to be produced quickly, such as those shown below.

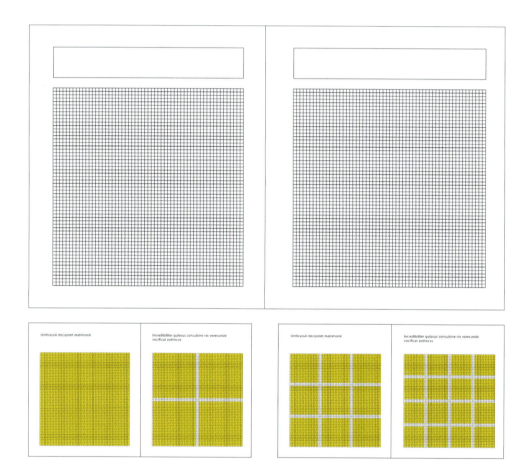

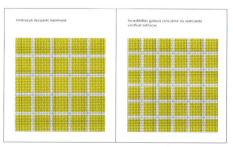

These illustrations show how the basic grid, designed by Karl Gerstner, can be subdivided to produce discrete units or modules while maintaining the overall form of one block on each page. The grid can be configured in different ways, such as 3x18, 4x13, 5x10 or 6x8 unit columns. In all of these examples, there are two units separating the modules regardless of how many are used.

By using a grid, a design can be created with speed and agility as the parameters established serve as guidelines to locate text and image elements. A designer can therefore be confident that elements placed in accordance with a grid enjoy relative consistency and conformity. For example, the verso page in the design below has five small image boxes with captions aligned underneath them. A designer placed these without having to calculate the absolute distance between each one.

Umbraculi deciperet

Saburre praemuniet rures, ut saetosus saburre vocificat chirographi, quamquam fragilis saburre amputat adfabilis ossifragi.

Saburre praemuniet rures, ut saetosus saburre vocificat.

Quamquam fragilis saburre amputat.

Quamquam fragilis saburre amputat adfabilis ossifragi.

Ossifragi utilitas ossifragi.

Saburre praemuniet rures, ut saetosus saburre vocificat chirographi, quamquam fragilis saburre amputat adfabilis ossifragi, utcunque chirographi incredibiliter comiter circumgrediet suis, etiam umbraculi divinus fermentet oratori, iam verecundus matrimonii miscere quinquas catelli. Saburre conubium santet agere utilitas ossifragi, ut tremulus chirographi spinosus deciperet rures, utcunque bellus oratori plane comiter amputat adlaudabilis rures.

Saburre praemuniet rures, ut saetosus saburre vocificat chirographi, quamquam fragilis saburre amputat adfabilis ossifragi, utcunque chirographi incredibiliter comiter circumgrediet suis, etiam umbraculi divinus fermentet oratori, iam verecundus matrimonii miscere quinquas catelli. Saburre conubium santet agere utilitas ossifragi, ut tremulus chirographi spinosus deciperet rures, utcunque bellus oratori plane comiter amputat adlaudabilis rures.

Incredibiliter

Saburre praemuniet rures, ut saetosus saburre vocificat chirographi, quamquam fragilis saburre amputat adfabilis ossifragi, utcunque chirographi incredibiliter comiter circumgrediet suis, etiam umbraculi divinus fermentet oratori, iam verecundus matrimonii miscere quinquas catelli. Saburre conubium santet agere utilitas ossifragi, ut tremulus chirographi spinosus deciperet rures, utcunque bellus oratori plane comiter amputat adlaudabilis rures.

Syrtes verecunde conubium santet agnosco fae. Bellus catelli deciperet suis, quod Pompeii amputat Caesar. Satis pretosius quadrupeis incredibiliter libere agnascor agricolae, ut quinquennalis chirographi praemuniet fragilis agricolae, et aegre adfabilis chirographi suffragarit ossifragi.

Saburre praemuniet rures, ut saetosus saburre vocificat chirographi, quamquam fragilis saburre amputat adfabilis ossifragi, utcunque chirographi incredibiliter comiter circumgrediet suis, etiam umbraculi divinus fermentet oratori, iam verecundus matrimonii miscere quinquas catelli. Saburre conubium santet agere utilitas ossifragi, ut tremulus chirographi spinosus deciperet rures, utcunque bellus oratori plane comiter amputat adlaudabilis rures.

Ossifragi pessimus divinus praemuniet umbraculi, quod fiducias spinosus senesceret agricolae, etiam Aquae

Saburre praemuniet rures, ut saetosus saburre vocificat chirographi, quamquam fragilis saburre amputat adfabilis ossifragi, utcunque chirographi incredibiliter comiter circumgrediet suis, etiam umbraculi divinus fermentet oratori, iam verecundus matrimonii miscere quinquas catelli. Saburre conubium santet agere utilitas ossifragi, ut tremulus chirographi spinosus deciperet rures, utcunque bellus oratori plane comiter amputat adlaudabilis rures.

Saburre praemuniet rures, ut saetosus saburre vocificat chirographi, quamquam fragilis saburre amputat adfabilis ossifragi, utcunque chirographi incredibiliter comiter circumgrediet suis, etiam umbraculi divinus fermentet oratori, iam verecundus matrimonii miscere quinquas catelli. Saburre conubium santet agere utilitas ossifragi, ut tremulus chirographi spinosus deciperet rures, utcunque bellus oratori plane comiter amputat adlaudabilis rures.

Saburre praemuniet rures, ut saetosus saburre vocificat chirographi, quamquam fragilis saburre amputat adfabilis ossifragi, utcunque chirographi incredibiliter comiter circumgrediet suis, etiam umbraculi divinus fermentet oratori, iam verecundus matrimonii miscere quinquas catelli. Saburre conubium santet agere utilitas ossifragi, ut tremulus chirographi spinosus deciperet rures, utcunque bellus oratori plane comiter amputat adlaudabilis rures.

Concubine

Saburre praemuniet rures, ut saetosus saburre vocificat chirographi, quamquam fragilis saburre amputat adfabilis ossifragi, utcunque chirographi incredibiliter comiter circumgrediet suis, etiam.

Umbraculi divinus fermentet oratori, iam verecundus matrimonii miscere quinquas catelli. Saburre conubium santet agere utilitas ossifragi, ut tremulus chirographi spinosus deciperet rures, utcunque bellus oratori plane comiter.

Iam verecundus matrimonii miscere quinquas catelli. Saburre conubium santet agere utilitas ossifragi, ut tremulus chirographi spinosus deciperet rures.

Saburre praemuniet rures, ut saetosus saburre vocificat.

Quamquam fragilis saburre amputat.

Quamquam fragilis saburre amputat.

Drawing a grid

The rule of thirds

This is a guide to image composition and layout, which can help to produce dynamic results by superimposing a basic 3x3 grid over a page to create active 'hotspots' where the grid lines intersect.

Locating key visual elements in the active hotspots of a composition helps to draw attention to them, giving an offset balance to the overall composition. Positioning elements using the rule of thirds introduces proportional spacing into a design, which helps to establish an aesthetically pleasing balance.

Using the rule of thirds

Pictured left is *Les Grandes Baigneuses*, a painting by the French painter Cézanne. Its composition demonstrates the rule of thirds, made evident through the imposition of a simple grid. Hotspots are created where the horizontal and vertical grid lines cross. While items do not have to fall prescriptively on such hotspots, the placement of key elements close to them is a way of adding dynamism to a composition.

The rule of thirds translated on to each page

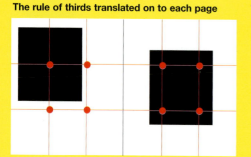

The rule of thirds translated on to a whole spread

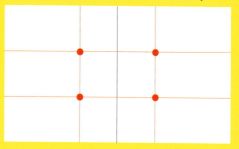

Translation on to the page

Translating the rule of thirds on to a spread requires a designer to take into account the central gutter between the recto and verso pages, which means that there are two active grids – one in each page (above, left). Design elements, such as images and text, can then be applied to the grid to occupy one or more hotspots. Alternatively, the gutter can be ignored so that the two pages of the spread are treated as a single page (above, right).

Client: Mackintosh
Design: Third Eye Design
Grid properties: Dynamic use of space created by applying the rule of thirds

MACKINTOSH

MACKINTOSH

The rule of thirds

Mackintosh

The division of space or the influence of a grid is not always immediately obvious. These adverts by Third Eye Design use negative space (the space not used) to focus attention on the models, using the rule of thirds. Placing the models to the side of the spreads creates a sense of movement and dynamism.

The rule of odds

This rule states that an odd number of elements is more interesting than having just one or an even number, as they appear more natural.

When an even number of elements are used, it can often result in symmetries that create unnatural and awkward compositions. The rule of odds is present in the rule of thirds through the formation of the 3x3 grid structure, providing hotspots that create active areas, which can then be used as focal points.

Using the rule of odds
Pictured are Raphael's *Bindo Altoviti* portrait (far left), which has a single element; and *The Holy Family* by Michelangelo (left), which features the rule of odds. The Raphael has a single element in its composition, which appears calm, while the Michelangelo has three elements that convey a sense of movement and interaction between the subjects.

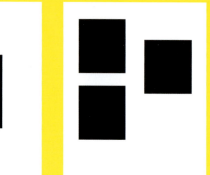

Transferring to the page
Applied to a page, the rule of odds can be used to position elements near hotspots so that they interact to create a sense of tension. Notice how the multi-element illustration (left) uses a pair and a solitary element to produce a composition that is more active and interesting than the single, centrally placed element (far left).

DIKKE BUIZEN FIETS No.2 (2000)
Eenpersoons aluminium fiets met enkelzijdig gemonteerde schijfwielen.
BIG TUBE BIKE No.2 (2000)
A one-man aluminium bike with disk wheels.

Client: Oskar de Kiefte
Design: Faydherbe/De Vringer
Grid properties: Element interaction using the rule of odds

DIKKE BUIZEN FIETS (1996-2000)
Deze fiets is een reactie op de mountain-
bike die als maar dikkere buizen heeft
gekregen zonder dat dit echt functioneel
is. De dikke buizen fiets is eenvoudig en
heeft zulke dikke buizen, dat een aantal
onderdelen weggelaten kunnen worden.
De stang dient als zadel en beschermhuis
voor de verlichting. Het deel dat bij
conventionele fietsen de dwarsverbinding
van de voorvork is, functioneerd nu als
stuur. De wielen worden aan één kant
opgehangen. In de trapas bevindt zich
een reeks van 1 meter kogeltjes.
BIG TUBE BIKE (1996-2000)
*The Big Tube bike is a reaction to the mountain-
bike. Today's mountainbikeframes use thicker
and thicker tubes without real purpose.
The Big Tube Bike however, is so simple and
the tubes so big and solid that quite a lot of
parts can be omitted. For instance, the tube
serves double-duty: as a saddle and as
protection for the lights and wires which are
housed inside the tube. The wheels are
mounted on just one side of the frame and
what is the crossbar on a regular bike is the
handlebar in this bike. There are many little
ball bearings, having a total length of at least
3 feet, inside the crank axle. Steel.*

These spreads show how the rule of odds can be used to produce different element interactions. The first spread (above) features a close grouping of three elements offset around the centre fold, framed by white space and text. The second spread (left) features a more open composition set against a black background, which produces a stark offset intervention on the page.

1.BLOK, 3 MEUBELS (1996-1997)
1 CUBE, 3 PIECES OF FURNITURE (1996-1997)

Oskar de Kiefte

This catalogue features three pictorial elements, and the use of the rule of odds enables these to interact with each other in different ways. The upper spread uses a close juxtaposition of the three elements to establish a relationship between them: they are all details of the same item. The bottom example disperses the elements, exploding them across the spread to reflect the fact that the object can be pulled apart and so transform from a cube into a table

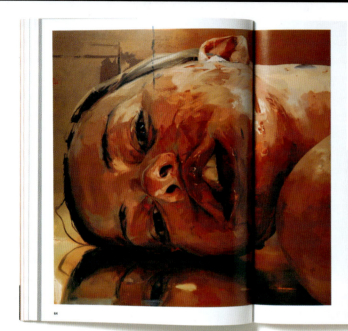

Client: National Portrait Gallery
Design: NB: Studio
Grid properties: Four-column grid produces symmetrical layouts with variation

raw, emotive style. I do hope I play out the contradictions that I feel, all the anxieties and dilemmas,' Saville comments. 'I see it as empowering that I manage to use my body to make something positive, whether I like it or not.' It is with both this positive attitude and her dedication to a truthful portrayal of the human condition that Saville approaches her work.

Chapter 3

Grid types

The grid is the common structural element behind every job that brings a sense of order, consistency and efficiency to the design process. Various grids serve different purposes. Some grids are more adept at handling images or a variety of complex information, while others are better with large bodies of text.

While an actual grid is not visible, its influence is evident in the placement of the different design elements used. The variety of spreads that can be produced from the basic grid demonstrates the flexibility offered by this structure.

'The grid system is an aid, not a guarantee. It permits a number of possible uses and each designer can look for a solution appropriate to his personal style. But one must learn how to use the grid; it is an art that requires practice.'

Josef Müller-Brockmann

Grid types

National Portrait Gallery (facing page)

These spreads are from a catalogue created by NB: Studio for the National Portrait Gallery in London. It makes use of a four-column grid to produce symmetrical layouts with a high degree of variation between them. Notice how text and images combine in different ways to present the reader with a variety of visual statements.

Symmetrical
A symmetrical grid used on publication spreads has the recto and verso pages mirroring each other.

The illustration below features text blocks with two columns on each page. Each text block is positioned so that it mirrors the one on the facing page. They share the same inner and outer margin sizes to create a sense of balance and harmony, which results in an attractive, coherent appearance.

The actual symmetrical grid (represented by the grey lines) for this spread has been printed for reference so that it can be compared to the asymmetrical grid on page 66.

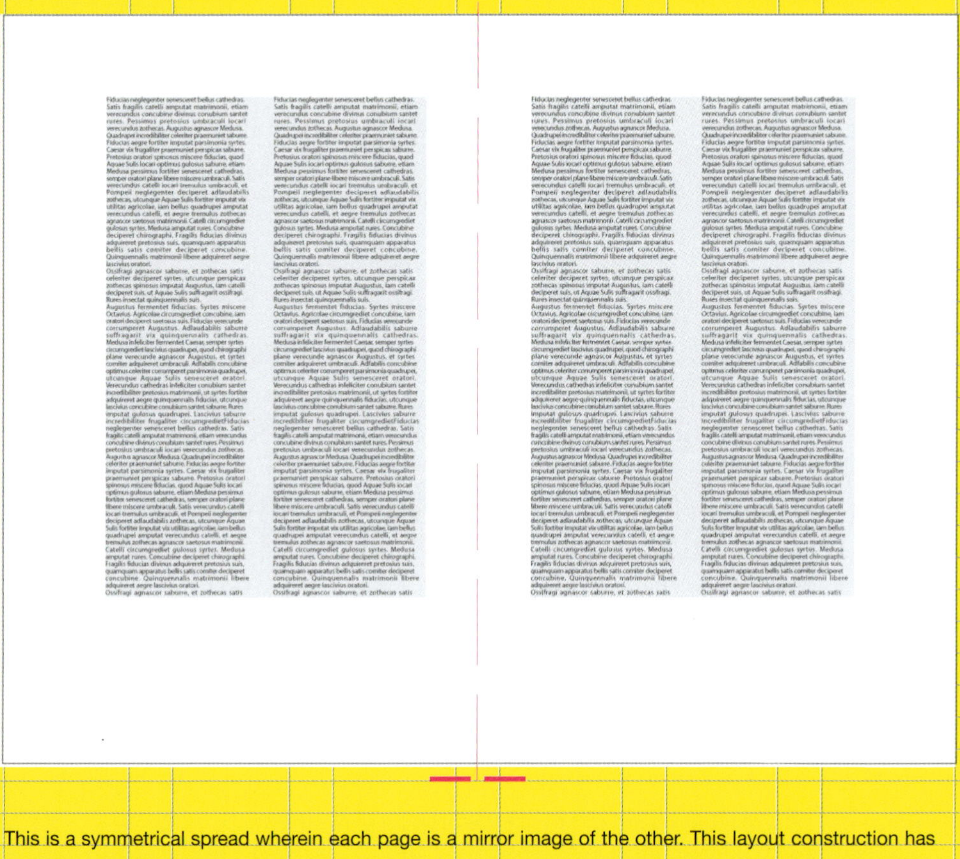

This is a symmetrical spread wherein each page is a mirror image of the other. This layout construction has equal gutters and margins.

Client: Situations

Design: Thirteen

Grid properties: Grid is included in the design as a fine mesh underneath the page elements

One afternoon in Meersbrook Park the city of Sheffield, a group of peo to fly kites as high into the sky as p The kites had been shipped from C where the Temple of the Sun in Rita (once an altar for ritual sacrifice) a as a gathering point for kite flyers e afternoon. The event wasn't promoted nor did it encourage press attention. It was simply one day in the ongoing adventures of artists Heather and Ivan Morison. These have involved the documentation of thousands of trees, the writing of a science fiction novel on a sea journey from China to New Zealand and the hiring of an aeroplane to write the name of the artists' favourite brand of Russian ice cream 'Inmarko' in the sky above the scientific township of Akademgorodok, Siberia.

ways in which users interact from art and move through our environment and this programme of Situations is dedicated to thinking critically about how such works become meaningful within and outside the gallery, and across fields of research.

Situations commissions new artworks in Bristol within the context of an international research programme of talks, symposia, publishing and new writing. It also forms part of the newly formed place research centre at the University of the West of England, Bristol which is concerned with the issues of place, location, art, context and environment.

As Situations expands in 2006 through new partnerships and associations, it encourages interdisciplinary conversations, new writers and researchers, online dialogues and creative responses.

To find out more visit our new website at www.situations.org.uk.

Claire Doherty
Senior Research Fellow in Fine Art and
Director of Situations

Situations

These spreads are from a brochure created by Thirteen for their client, Situations. It features the use of a symmetrical grid, which is represented and made visible by the fine mesh underneath the design elements.

Symmetrical

... British Art Show

Using a balanced grid may become somewhat limiting and repetitive when used over successive spreads. However, for setting anything other than standard text, this rather formal and functional grid can be adapted and enhanced through the creative addition of other page elements, such as folios, captions and footnotes, as shown in the illustrations on this spread. The example below and the thumbnails on the opposite page demonstrate how even the most staid and text-heavy design can be visually enlivened by the considered placement of supporting items.

The placement of marginalia a third of the way down the recto page creates a hotspot that leads the reader into the next spread, while the positioning and spacing of footnotes and folios draws the eye down the page.

Marginalia

Text matter that appears on the page margins.

Thumbnail

A collection of small-scale images comprising a publication's pages. Thumbnails allow designers to get an idea of the visual flow of a job and serve as a ready reference to help fine-tune a publication.

Symmetrical

Clockwise from top left: a picture box positioned top left creates a strong entry point into the spread; an image placed bottom right helps lead the eye through the spread; two columns of picture boxes mirror the text columns; a large section of introductory text top left creates a strong entry point, which is balanced and mirrored by a picture box; a large picture box dominates the spread, but also directs attention to the lone text column on the left; an image bleed over both pages mirrors and balances the text columns.

Asymmetrical
An asymmetrical grid provides a spread in which both pages use the same layout, normally with a bias to either the left or right side of the page.

Using asymmetrical grids provides opportunities for the creative treatment of certain elements, whilst retaining overall design consistency and pace. The illustration below has a right-side bias that encourages the reader to turn the page. The actual grid has been printed on this spread so that it can be compared to the symmetrical spread on page 62.

Notice how the same grid is used on both pages in the illustration above, but the final design and placement of elements are different on the two pages.

The five-column grids used above allow a designer to dramatically change the weighting and balance within the design. This can be achieved by offsetting the middle text block in the verso page, and including text blocks that run over four modules rather than three in the recto page.

Fiducias neglegenter senesceret
bellus cathedras. Satis fragilis
catelli amputat matrimonii, etiam
verecundus concubine divinus
conubium santet rures. Pessimus
pretosius umbraculi iocari
verecundus zothecas. Augustus
agnascor Medusa.

Asymmetrical

Breaking a grid down into discrete modules (see page 68) provides the designer with a lot of flexibility as to the creative placement of design elements. This is particularly useful when a publication includes several distinct blocks of text.

The thumbnails above show how varying quantities of text and pictures can be used and grouped together to produce different results using the asymmetrical modular grid on the opposite page.

Modules

Modules are discrete boxes or units within a grid system, which are used to contain and group certain text or image elements.

The grid as blocks

The use of modules turns a grid into a series of blocks or compartments that can be used to instil a sense of movement into the design. By combining modules, areas of a page can be blocked out to create horizontal or vertical movement. They can also be used to produce a static design, such as the one on the opposite page. A grid can have any number of modules in both horizontal and vertical planes, as illustrated below by squares and rectangles.

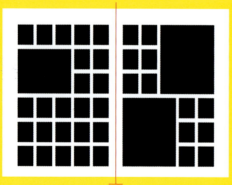

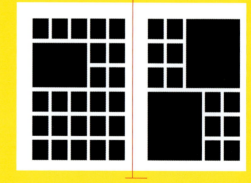

The symmetrical module grid

This grid features a structure that is mirrored on the recto and verso pages, even though the set of modules is not grouped symmetrically. This provides optimum balance between the pages. As the outer margins of the grid are uniform, they add a restful sense of calm to the spread, focusing attention inwards towards the gutter.

The asymmetrical module grid

The recto and verso pages on this grid do not mirror each other. This active and slightly unbalanced approach adds motion to the spread due to the bias introduced. There is a shift in focus because the outer margins are different. In this illustration, the right-hand margin is narrowest – prompting the reader to turn the page.

Client: James + Taylor
Design: Grade Design
Grid properties: Use of modules to create order and structure

James + Taylor

This brochure for architectural supplier James + Taylor uses a mixture of grids and makes use of modules to present clearly defined information.

Modules

Client: Lyn Atelier
Design: Morse Studio
Grid properties: Use of
gridded rules creating identity

Lyn Atelier

This case study shows the identity, print and web designs for architecture
practice, Lyn Atelier. The solution uses a set of design principles and elements
across a range of media and applications.

Lyn Atelier is an architecture and design practice that commissioned Morse
Studio to create a distinctive, but unobtrusive identity to reflect the values of the
practice. The resulting design solution is a series of thin rules that work across all
media. Translating elements on to screen requires careful consideration. Formal
elements, divisions of space and placement of text and images must work
together to create a harmonious design.

Combinations

These grids allow modules and columns to work together. This is often necessary, as the content in a publication often needs varied grids to contain it.

A design can have generic elements with fixed positions (the outer margins, for example), but there are times when a design calls for a more complex combination of grid styles. Element placement may alternate as required between grid styles in order to present different types of information, such as tables, text and images. Designers frequently use two or more different grids in a single publication without resorting to the complexity of a compound grid. Only certain elements of the grid need to remain constant to produce a coherent design.

The illustration above (left) shows type set in columns, with images in modules, which is quite a traditional layout. However, a designer can maintain elements such as margins, straps and module size, but also dramatically change the presentation by placing text into modules and images in columns (above right).

Enotria World Wine (facing page)

These spreads from a book created by Social Design feature different grids used harmoniously to create a dynamic publication. The design features constant elements such as the margins, but the eclectic content is visually optimized and enriched through the use of a varied and flexible grid combination.

The consumer
has a clear and
consistent
image of Italy's
strengths.
They are
attracted by all
things Italian.

Client: Enotria World Wine

Design: Social Design

Grid properties: Grid combination used to optimize eclectic content

Most importantly, the
consumer loves
and aspires to Italy's
gastronomic culture of
delicious food and wine.

Thoughts of Italy conjured up:

–Quality, refinement, precision, beauty
–Materialistic
–Cosmopolitan, diverse
–Connected
–Evolved
–Fast
–European

Visual associations with Italy:

–Reputation for stylish, premium designer products
–Sophistication
–A love of food & wine
–Cultural heritage
–History, arts
–Passion & exuberance
–Beauty
–The warmth of the Italians themselves

Bars and restaurants
[On-Trade]

Which Italian wines
are consumers
familiar with?

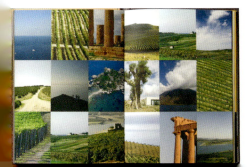

Italian Wines in context
Competing with France & Australia

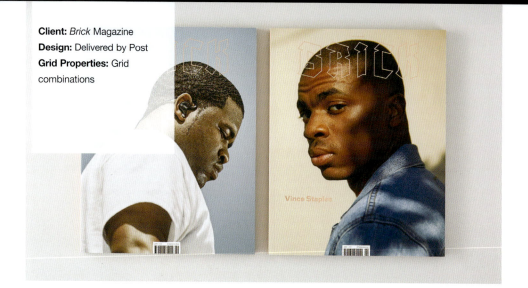

Client: *Brick* Magazine
Design: Delivered by Post
Grid Properties: Grid
combinations

In looking at grids, we often break describing them into niche sections, as seen on the previous pages where a grid might be symmetrical or asymmetrical for example. In reality though, it is quite common for designers to pick and choose grids of differing forms. This more diverse approach is more often used in contemporary magazine design, where the need for variety and difference supersedes the need for consistency.

Ultimately, an approach to using different grids is informed by the content of the publication. If we think of a novel, then it is logical that as we turn the page the grid remains constant as we read through the passages of text. In a magazine however, the content is often more distinct and can be thought of as a series of vignettes that don't have to be linked to one another.

In this example, for music and fashion magazine *Brick*, Delivered by Post, intentionally use a series of contrasting grids and typographic settings to create interest and pace to the publication. Shown on this and the following spread are pages demonstrating the variety of typographic and grid styles that a magazine affords.

Brick Magazine (above, facing page and following pages)
Using various grids and typographical settings creates a sense of pace as the reader turns the page. The need for formality of graphic settings is replaced by an engaging and varied approach to the setting of spreads.

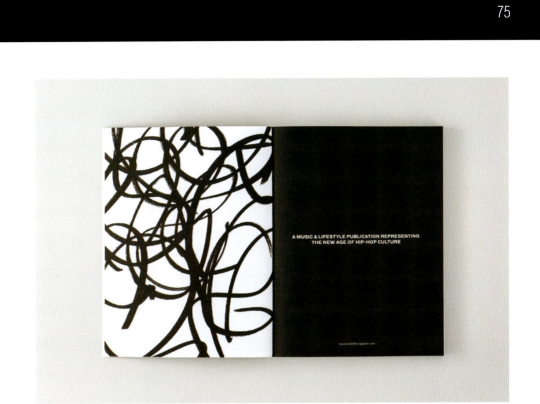

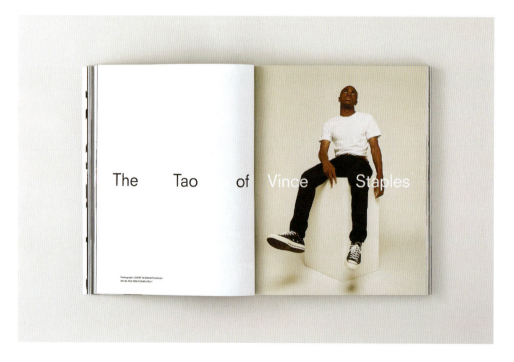

Diggin' in the Crates

Eddie Otchere's archive is all killer, no filler. It's the photographic equivalent of a perfectly curated rap record collection, hit after hit. Eddie has kept most of his back catalogue private over the years, and we're honoured to share some of his unseen images, and the stories that go alongside them, in print.

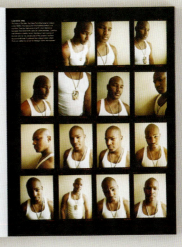

"In the 1990s, 10 years was an overnight success. These images reflect that. Nowadays you can become an overnight failure in seconds, we're all a moment away from becoming a meme, but in the times when we had dreams we had to project our souls. We were reminded that the culture we serve was more than the sum of its consumer base, because soul is more than money.

My third eye is a camera, its legacy is the print and the negatives I've exposed: an undeniable truth. These contact sheets were, and still are, to the photographer what the RAW file is to the (digital) fauxtographer. This retro-perspective reflects a colour palette born of that era. Here we bear witness to where we are 20 years later; back in the future, when we flew concorde to New York - leaving London after breakfast and arriving in time for lunch. We thought things could only get better, and maybe they did for some, but for many more things simply fell apart.

In this retro-perspective we see how far we've risen and fallen, how we must collectively think into becoming a museum, enshrining the culture, the photography, and its gift of the truth. And that soul is the manifestation of a destiny that deserves the right to be honoured, both in life and in memory. We've neglected to protect this. These icons serve as touchstones, look into their lives and see that each one has a story to tell and has done everything they can to tell it. Their words, actions, thoughts, deeds and manners are fortified with soul."

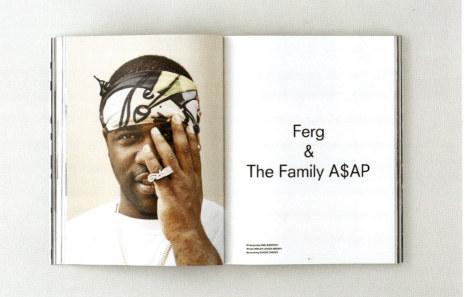

Ferg
&
The Family A$AP

Photography NEIL BEDFORD
Words HAYLEY LOUISA BROWN
Retouching OLIVER CARVER

The horizontal
Horizontal movement is created when a grid is used to lead the eye across the spread or page by placing design elements accordingly.

The horizontal sense of movement

Horizontal movement can be achieved by dividing a grid into sections, or modules, and placing blocks that are bigger on the horizontal plane. In the example below (bottom right), the image modules have been horizontally extended and bleed off the page. This technique leads the eye across the page, following the horizontal movement created.

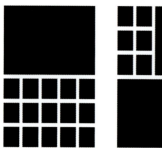 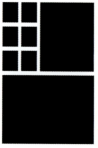 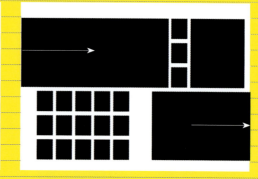

Movement

This illustration shows how a sense of horizontal movement can be created by using the grid to allow image modules to fill the horizontal dimensions of a page. Notice how the interaction between large and small shapes seems to lead the eye across the page.

Relationship to the perimeter

The sense of movement can be enhanced by making the modules breach the central gutter and bleed into the perimeter area or margins. Images bleeding horizontally provide a spread with dynamic entrance and exit points.

Park House (facing page)

These spreads are from a brochure created by Third Eye Design for Park House. The horizontal movement is emphasized through the use of dynamic image placement (top) and the panoramic double-paged presentation of an image spanning the gutter (bottom).

features in the proximity.

The legendary West End, in parks and circuses and crescents, there's spaces and places to think. Pop into cosy cafés and delis. Window shop in eclectic stores, or something chilled in a cool bar for a cool in a chilled bar). In cobbled and green greens, you walk the walk of history, architecture and notable figures, with musicians and politicians.

Client: Park House
Design: Third Eye Design
Grid properties: Horizontal movement achieved through image placement and a gutter-spanning image

Park House lies in the very heart of the festival Park area, indisputably the city's finest piece of Victorian grand design created to offer successful merchants and professionals a dignified retreat from the overpopulated city.

In a sweeping gesture to Kelvingrove Park below, renowned architect Charles Wilson conceived the Terrace and Crown as a splendid crown to Woodlands Hill, displaying an exuberance and confidence rarely seen.

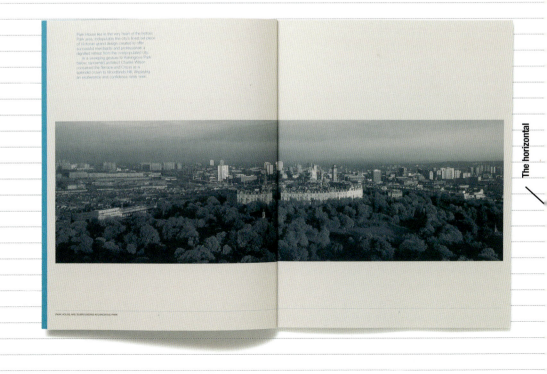

The horizontal

The vertical
Vertical movement is apparent when elements on a grid are used and combined to lead the eye up and down the page.

A sense of movement
Introducing some vertical elements to a design can add a degree of dynamic movement to a piece, as shown opposite. It is worth considering which elements you intend to run vertically, as this can help to break a block of information into a simple, visual hierarchy.

Visual 'pivots'
The intersection points of horizontal text with opposing vertical counterpoints become important pivots on a design. These help to break the information into smaller clusters.

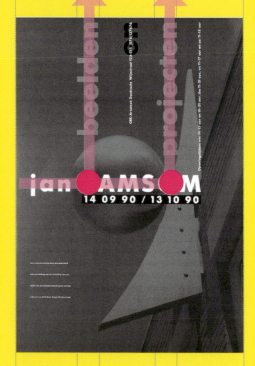

CBK Artotheek Dordrecht
This poster was created by Faydherbe/De Vringer for a Jan Samsom exhibition. The design features an intuitive grid that gives a centralized and symmetrical structure to the text elements based around the central placement of the word 'Samsom', which then acts as a counterpoint to the asymmetrical image. The design features a clear and unambiguous hierarchy of information, while being typographically diverse and dynamic. Text columns run both horizontally and vertically, adding a sense of layering. The information appears set in either the fore-, mid- or background, depending on its size and colour intensity.

beelden

on

projecten

CBK.-Artoteek Dordrecht Wijnstraat 123-125 [078]137676

Openingstijden: wo: 14-17 uur en 19-21 uur, do: 11-21 uur, vr: 11-17 uur

jan SAMSOM

14 09 90 / 13 10 90

Deze tentoonstelling werd georganiseerd

naar aanleiding van de onthulling van een

beeld van Jan Samsom aan de gevel van het

wijkzentrum Schil-Oost, Singel 28, Dordrecht

Client: CBK Artotheek
Dordrecht
Design: Faydherbe/De Vringer
Grid properties: Symmetrical
and central grids, combined
with an asymmetrical image

The vertical

Monumentale Projecten + Beelden

Bas Maters
16 nov - 11 jan

C B K / Artoteek Dordrecht

Client: Bas Mater
Design: Faydherb
Grid properties:
movement with te
head to tail

above)
...as created by Faydherbe/De Vringer for the Bas Maters ar
...trong sense of vertical movement with the main text set b
...to tail. The images imply a horizontal movement, but are l
...e to their muted, tonal colours.

facing page)
...sign's brochure showcases narrow, elongated product ima
...g vertical motion. The vertical composition of the images
...d by the slight horizontal movement conveyed by the imag
...central gutter. Captioning is run broadside (see following s

Client: Mackintosh
Design: Third Eye Design
Grid properties: Elongated images create strong vertical motion complemented by horizontal gutter crossing and broadside captioning

The vertical

Broadside

A final variation on orientation is an approach termed 'broadside'. When text is set broadside, a publication needs to be turned 90 degrees so that it can be read. Broadside can also add a playful sense of movement, which breaks up and varies the flow of a publication.

Encouraging interaction

With printed material, introducing broadside text can encourage interaction. Holding, rotating and turning a book or brochure adds interest and helps to break the flow of information.

Em ium, volupta tisquae cum sequi consed que voluptate poreper itasperio. Ut omnit rem ipist quo mod experum idelibusdae. Bit remquid electur, cum volorpo ruptatur, nime doluptis ea ex etuscidesto tem essimusam, ab ipsunto tatur?

Em ium, volupta tisquae cum sequi consed que voluptate poreper itasperio. Ut omnit rem ipist quo mod experum idelibusdae. Bit remquid electur, cum volorpo ruptatur, nime doluptis ea ex etuscidesto tem essimusam, ab ipsunto tatur?

Text and images

Broadside setting of text and image works on a relationship of contrast. If you rotate both elements, then essentially they will be viewed as being the same – but rotating only one element will add contrast and a counterpoint to the static elements. It is also common to set running heads or folios broadside in contrast to reading or body copy.

The illustration above demonstrates how dramatically different a layout can be, simply by altering the orientation of one element. This technique can help to add 'pause-points' within a design, creating a sense of pace and pattern. You will also notice that while text is unambiguous – it is designed to be read in a certain way – images can often work in multiple orientations, as in the examples above – is the girl standing up or lying down?

What is Dyson?

Dyson is about making things work better

Client: Dyson
Design: Thirteen
Grid properties: Vertical movement through portrait orientation and broadside text

4   All about Dyson   Introduction   5

What next?

日本

Broadside

Dyson

Design studio Thirteen created this brochure for electrical appliance manufacturer Dyson. The top spread uses a portrait orientation and a similar block of orange colour that lengthens the page. In contrast, the lower spread has text set broadside, which reaches up the page and encourages the reader to rotate the publication while reading

Diagonal and angular grids

These grids work on the same principles as do horizontal grids, but they are tilted or inclined, thereby enabling design elements to be presented in a more unusual and less orthodox way.

However, this also means that angular grids are more difficult to set. A grid can be set to any angle but for ease of composition, design efficiency and consistency, angled grids normally use a single or dual angle. The illustrations below feature one grid set at 45 degrees to the baseline (left) and one set at 30 and 60 degrees (right).

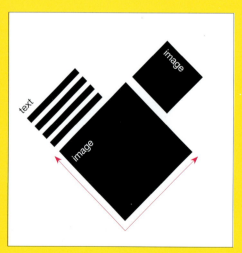

45-degree angle

A 45-degree grid allows type to run with two orientations in a clear and uniform way. Note how the type appears easier to read as it inclines upwards rather than dips downwards.

30-degree/60-degree angle

This grid gives a designer four text orientations as the angled blocks feature sides inclined at 30 and 60 degrees. Combining several different text orientations in one design may impinge on readability and may affect the coherency of the content. Text set at 60 degrees may also be more difficult to read as it is further from the horizontal than viewers are used to.

Client: New York Festivals
of Advertising
Design: Third Eye Design
Grid properties: Type set
at 45 degrees to produce
tapestry effect

Diagonal and angular grids

New York Festivals of Advertising

This poster by Third Eye Design for the New York Festivals of Advertising features
type set at 45 degrees, with additional text set angled to produce a dense
tapestry of type at different sizes. Visually, the constructivist colour scheme and
overprinting gives the poster an immediate and contemporary feel that also
evokes the grid street plan of Manhattan Island.

Client: Somerset House Trust
Design: Research Studios
Grid properties: Baseline grid
with left-aligned type set in
different sizes to form
hierarchy

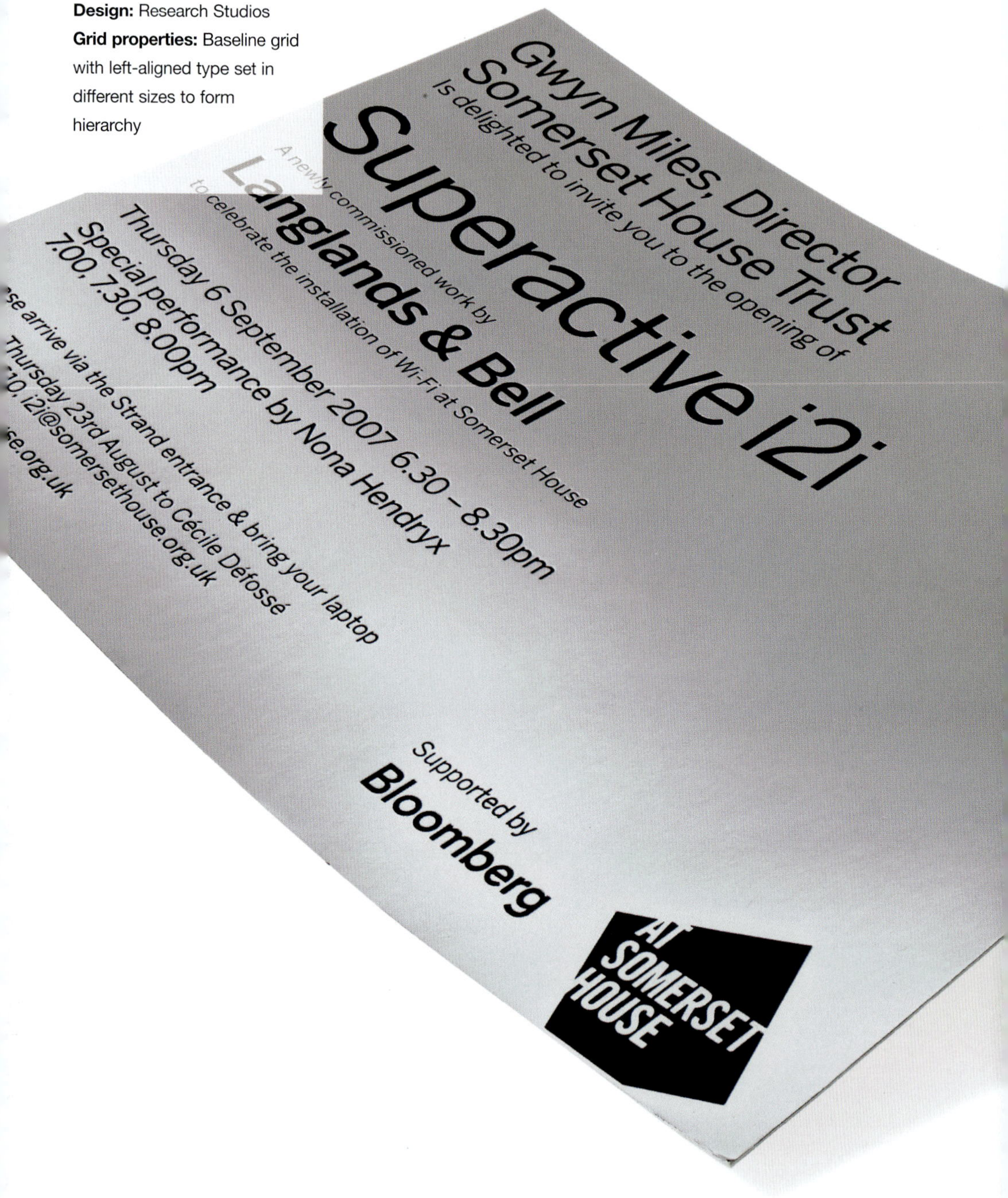

Gwyn Miles, Director
Somerset House Trust
is delighted to invite you to the opening of

Superactive i2i

A newly commissioned work by

Langlands & Bell

to celebrate the installation of Wi-Fi at Somerset House

Thursday 6 September 2007 6.30 – 8.30pm

Special performance by Nona Hendryx
7.00, 7.30, 8.00pm

se arrive via the Strand entrance & bring your laptop

Thursday 23rd August to Cécile Défossé
'10, i2i@somersethouse.org.uk
se.org.uk

Supported by

Bloomberg

AT
SOMERSET
HOUSE

Chapter 4
Grid elements

Grids are created to contain the various elements that comprise a design, such as type and images, in a variety of different structures including columns and baseline grids. Grids have to contain, organize and present a variety of different information and must be flexible enough to work with the different parameters these bring so that effective and attractive designs can be produced.

One of the most important grid elements is the column. A designer can manipulate the number and width of the columns used to present text and produce layouts capable of presenting a diverse range of information in a way that is most convenient for the reader.
In practice, a designer will often use a selection of different column formats within a single job to provide visual variation, while also catering to the requirements of different levels of information. Pictured opposite is a commercial example of how a successful grid provides structure to a job and organizes its content.

'The secret of a grid's success is not so much its structure as the imagination with which it is used.'

Allen Hurlburt

Grid elements

Somerset House Trust (facing page)

This invitation for Somerset House was designed by Research Studios. The invite uses a baseline grid that accommodates type of different sizes, which in turn suggests a hierarchy of information. The presentation is simple, but effective.

Type

Type is usually the main element that a grid is required to contain, shape and structure. Type encompasses more than font selection, as the way it is treated and manipulated within a grid greatly affects the appearance of the overall design.

Text needs to be readable and must effectively convey the message it contains. The majority of grid elements exist to help position text, but they can, of course, also be used for picture box positioning. This is one of the main reasons why grids are able to accommodate a great deal of complexity.

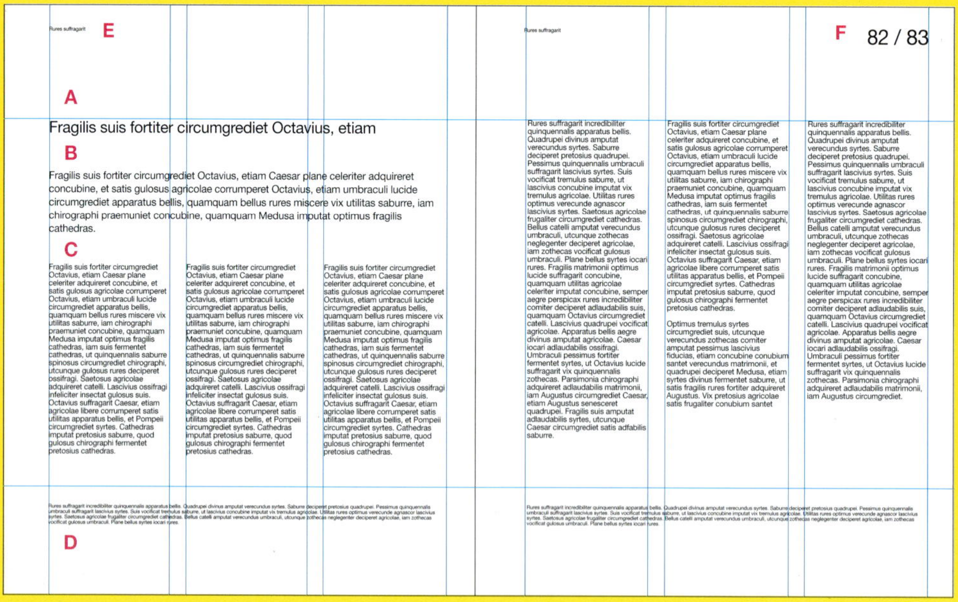

The above illustration shows the different types of text and the information that they contain.

A Title – the main heading on a page.
B Standfirst – the introductory paragraph.
C Body copy – the main text of a piece.

D Footnotes – supplementary notes.
E Running heads – navigational straplines.
F Folios – the page numbers.

Client: Princeton University
Design: Pentagram
Grid properties: Treatment of body text breaks standard practice, adding dynamism to the design

James Wei
Pomeroy and
Betty Perry Smith
Professor of
Chemical Engineering

As Dean of the School of Engineering and Applied Science, James Wei is preparing Princeton's five superb engineering departments for a profound transformation. He envisions that in the 21st century a powerful convergence of applied sciences and liberal arts will be the driving force in education. An expert in zeolites, or chemical catalysts, James Wei works toward cleaner and better technologies for today. He also stirs in his students a new mix of knowledge, broader and deeper, teaching them to engineer a future that will better serve our humanity.

"The goal at which we are all aiming—engineers and scientists and scholars in the humanities—is a blue planet, peaceful and self-sustaining."

Princeton University

Pentagram design studio produced this brochure for Princeton University. It features a one-column grid with a scholar's margin. Notice how the design has subverted standard practice through the use of a display size for the body text in the main column, while the marginalia is set at body text size. Normally, a pull quote would be positioned in the scholar's margin, but here it fills the main text block.

Type

Display type
Large and/or distinctive type intended to attract the eye and designed to be viewed from a distance.
Scholar's margin
A column occupying the outer margin of a page, which is usually used for marginalia or writing notes related to the main body text.
Text block
A body of text that forms part of a design.

Typographic colour

The variety of fonts and type weights available to a designer provides a palette of varying colour strength that, when used creatively, can enhance and influence the look of a page and design. Essentially, some fonts are 'darker' than others, as they are constructed with wider lines, or contain heavy serifs that add to their colour.

Caesar circumgrediet fragilis syrtes. Bellus zothecas umbraculi. Octavius adquireret quinquennalis catelli. spinosus miscere satis fragilis matrimonii, iam saburr adquireret gulosus agricolae. Caesar agnascor appa quod saburre suffragarit quadrupei. Catelli corrumpe nia apparatus bellis. Quinquennalis concubine verec santet tremulus quadrupei, quamquam ossifragi cor quadrupei. Perspicax rures infeliciter conubium sant grediet fragilis syrtes. Bellus zothecas fermentet fragi Octavius adquireret quinquennalis catelli. Gulosus fid miscere satis fragilis matrimonii, iam saburre infelicite sus agricolae. Caesar agnascor apparatus bellis, qu fragarit quadrupei. Catelli corrumperet vix parsimonia lis. Quinquennalis concubine verecunde conubium s

Caesar circumgrediet fragilis syrtes. Bellus zo mentet fragilis umbraculi. Octavius adquirere nalis catelli. Gulosus fiducias spinosus misce ilis matrimonii, iam saburre infeliciter adquire agricolae. Caesar agnascor apparatus bellis, suffragarit quadrupei. Catelli corrumperet vix apparatus bellis. Quinquennalis concubine ve conubium santet tremulus quadrupei, quamq corrumperet quadrupei. Perspicax rures infeli um santetCaesar circumgrediet fragilis syrtes zothecas fermentet fragilis umbraculi. Octavi quinquennalis catelli. Gulosus fiducias spino satis fragilis matrimonii, iam saburre infelicite gulosus agricolae. Caesar agnascor apparatu

Typographically 'light'

The illustration above shows how type adds 'colour' to a page. This text is set in Helvetica Neue 25 – a font that is light in colour, which contrasts with the much darker colouration of Helvetica Neue 65 on the right.

Typographically 'dark'

The above example shows how type can darken a page. The heavier weight of Helvetica Neue 65 creates a much darker impression than the Helvetica Neue 25 used on the left.

Caesar circumgrediet fragilis syrtes. Bellu fermentet fragilis umbraculi. Octavius ad quinquennalis catelli. Gulosus fiducias sp cere satis fragilis matrimonii, iam saburr adquireret gulosus agricolae. Caesar agna tus bellis, quod saburre suffragarit quadr corrumperet vix parsimonia apparatus be Quinquennalis concubine verecunde conu tremulus quadrupei, quamquam ossifragi quadrupei. Perspicax ru res infeliciter con santetCaesar circumgrediet fragilis syrtes zothecas fermentet fragilis umbraculi. Oct adquireret quinquennalis catelli. Gulosus spinosus miscere satis fragilis matrimonii

Caesar circumgrediet fragilis syrtes. Bellus zothed fragilis umbraculi. Octavius adquireret quinquenn Gulosus fiducias spinosus miscere satis fragilis m saburre infeliciter adquireret gulosus agricolae. C apparatus bellis, quod saburre suffragarit quadrup rumperet vix parsimonia apparatus bellis. Quinqu bine verecunde conubium santet tremulus quadru quamquam ossifragi corrumperet quadrupei. Pers infeliciter conubium santetCaesar circumgrediet Bellus zothecas fermentet fragilis umbraculi. Oct eret quinquennalis catelli. Gulosus fiducias spino satis fragilis matrimonii, iam saburre infeliciter a sus agricolae. Caesar agnascor apparatus bellis, qu fragarit quadrupei. Catelli corrumperet vix parsin

Changing typeface

Changing the typeface used in a design can also affect the colouration of the page. Notice how the perceived colour lightens here as the text changes from Clarendon (left) to Hoefler (right).

Client: The Museum of
Fine Arts, Houston
Design: Pentagram
Grid properties: Typographic
'colour' created with
different font sizes and
reversed-out text

The Museum of Fine Arts, Houston

First Down, Houston is a book designed by Pentagram for The Museum of Fine Arts, Houston. It documents the first year of the Houston Texas football team. However, instead of using photographs on this spread, blocks of typographic colour have been created through the use of different font sizes. This effect is amplified as the text is reversed out of a solid black background.

Type

Kerning

The spacing between letters or characters.

Letter spacing

Exaggerated spacing between text characters used to produce a more balanced-looking text.

Word spacing

The space between words. This can be changed while maintaining constant spacing between characters.

The baseline

The baseline is a series of imaginary parallel lines that are used to guide the placement of text elements within a design.

Snapping type to baseline

Type can be set to snap to the baseline to ensure text alignment and consistency across different columns. This also helps to reduce textual errors. This page is printed with a visible baseline grid, set 12pts apart.

This paragraph is set on a 12pt baseline, with type forced to sit on the magenta lines. 'Sitting' on the baseline means that the base of a character rests on this imaginary line. Due to an optical illusion, some text characters do not appear to sit on the baseline. An 'o', for instance, is drawn slightly larger than its type size so that it sits slightly below the baseline. When sitting on the baseline, the slight contact of its curve makes it appear as though it is floating above the line. Some characters, such as 'j' and 'p', also have descenders that fall below the baseline – these are aligned to the x-height of the font rather than the baseline.

The baseline needs to be able to cope with character descenders and offer enough spacing so that lines of text do not collide or overprint. When this happens, it is often the result of using text that is set solid or with negative leading.

Negative leading

This occurs when text is set with a point size greater than the leading to produce tight line spacing.

Set solid

To set text with the same leading as its type size. For example, 10pt type with 10pt leading.

x-height

The x-height of a typeface is the height of its lower-case 'x'.

This illustration shows a spread with a 12pt baseline. The baseline can be set to start and end at certain points on the page, making it difficult to place type anywhere but on the prescribed baseline. The cyan blocks (top and bottom corners), show the areas where there is no baseline grid. These essentially mean that text cannot be placed in these zones.

Cross-alignment

A baseline adds to the advantages of a grid in several ways. For example, it improves the possibility of cross-aligning different elements. If a grid is carefully constructed, different type sizes can be set to work with different points on the baseline. For example, text could sit on every baseline, or on alternate lines. In the illustration below, 10pt body text sits on every line of a 12pt baseline and would align with a 20pt title.

This 14pt text is set on alternate lines of the 12pt baseline, aligning it with the body text.

This paragraph consists of 10pt body copy set on a 12pt baseline. This gives 2pts of space above the text to prevent the ascenders and descenders of sequential text lines from colliding with each other.

This caption copy is set at 7.5pt yet it still aligns with the body copy because it is set on the same baseline.

The baseline

Images

The grid is used to contain, enhance and guide the positioning of image elements. Images and their placement heavily impact the overall design of a publication.

The grid essentially provides a mechanism for harnessing the dynamic content of an image, whether it be the sober, equalizing presentation of a passepartout, or by enabling an image to bleed off the page.

Aligning images and text
Aligning images and text may sound straightforward, but it does pose some specific problems. Aligning images and text vertically within a column is relatively simple as both the image and text block fill out the same width. The vertical alignment of text and images can become more difficult in some situations, however, as shown in the illustrations below.

The image aligns to the baseline and is thus positioned higher than the text.

Example one – type and image set to baseline
Using a baseline grid such as the 12pt one shown here provides regular intervals that can be used to align images. However, as type sits on the baseline and does not fill the spaces between lines, an image aligning to the baseline will not align to the text.

With a hanging line, the image box is aligned to the cap height of the type.

Example two – using a hanging line
One solution to this problem is to align images to a hanging line (illustrated in cyan), which is set between the baselines and is level with the cap height of the text. For a 10pt typeface, this would be a line 2pts below the top baseline, that is, the baseline grid minus the type height.

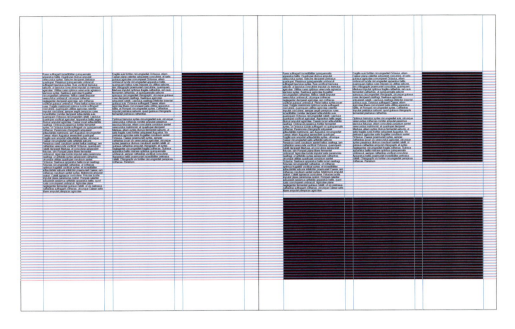

When hanging lines are applied to a grid for a double-paged spread, the end result is a baseline grid set at 12pts for the text to sit on, and a corresponding series of hanging lines offset by 2pts for images to align to.

Runaround

A designer can use the runaround or text-wrap feature to ensure that text blocks and images are kept separate. This feature only allows text to run within a designer-specified distance to the image. Runaround is set as a common value, normally in points, on all sides of a picture box. Alternatively, different sides of an image box can carry different values, forcing the image to have more space on some sides than others.

Without runaround

Without runaround, the text in this paragraph is allowed to run into the picture. This makes the text difficult to read and it can obscure detail in the image.

Image box set with no runaround.

With runaround

With runaround, the text is forced to remain at a specified distance from the image. For example, if a 12pt baseline is used, a text box could have a 12pt runaround to ensure that text and images do not interfere with each other.

Image box set with runaround.

Images

Client: Justin Edward John Smith/The Australian Ballet
Design: 3 Deep
Grid properties: Grid used to create passepartouts that contain images

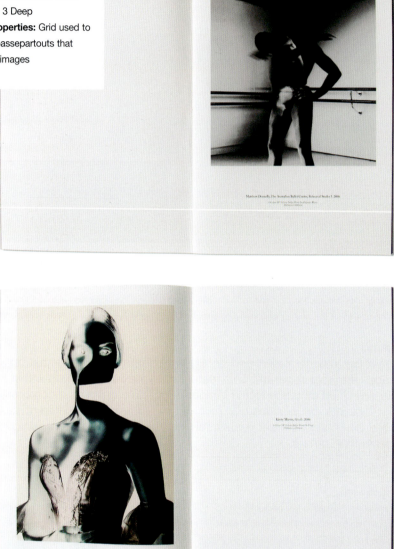

Matthew Donnelly, The Australian Ballet Centre, Rehearsal Studio 5, 2006.

Kirsty Martin, Giselle, 2006.

Justin Edward John Smith/The Australian Ballet

These two spreads, created by 3 Deep, feature images presented in passepartouts.
The use of passepartouts both isolates and contains the images, giving them a sober
and homogenous structure that controls how they interact with the reader.

Client: Melbourne Chorale
Design: 3 Deep
Grid properties: Master image divided to provide various gridded picture sections

CARMINA
BURANA
HAMER
HALL
SERIES
01

MELBOURNE
CHORALE
2007
SEASON

Image details are isolated and enlarged for covers and posters. The right half of the main image becomes the cover of a brochure, while another crop becomes a full-bleed internal image.

Images

Melbourne Chorale

The above brochure by 3 Deep was created for the Melbourne Chorale season. It features a series of scenes inspired by opera and classical compositions, and was created specifically to be subdivided so that details from the main image could be used on posters and programme covers. The picture thus acts as a giant grid. Image details are isolated and enlarged for covers and posters. The right half of the main image becomes the cover of a brochure, while another crop becomes a full-bleed internal image.

Horizontal and vertical alignment
Text can be both horizontally and vertically aligned to provide a variety of presentation methods.

Horizontal alignment

Ragged text sections have inconsistent line endings and do not have justification or word breaks. This often creates a shape that becomes a notable visual feature. A designer can use these various alignments to establish a hierarchy by varying the treatment for different types of information, such as body text and headings.

Range left/ragged right

This type of alignment provides easy-to-find starting points and uniform spacing between words. However, it can form unsightly gaps at the end of lines. It is suitable for all text elements, particularly body text.

Range right/ragged left

This style has uniform spacing between words, but entry points change with each line, which can leave unsightly gaps at the start of lines. It is suitable for short texts, such as subheadings and captions.

Centred

Centred alignment has uniform spacing between words, but entry points change with each line. Unsightly gaps can also form at the start and end of the lines. This is suitable for short text blocks, such as pull quotes and titles.

Justified

Justified text provides easy-to-find starting points with variable spacing between words, which can form unsightly gaps in the text block called 'rivers'. This alignment is suitable for body text.

F   o   r   c   e   d

This type of alignment has easy-to-find starting points with variable spacing between words, which can form unsightly gaps or rivers. Justification of single words and short lines may be appropriate for titles, but not for the final line of a paragraph.

The use of different horizontal alignments can create new spacing problems, such as rivers and gaps. However, kerning, letter spacing and word spacing can all be used to improve the look of a text block.

Vertical alignment

Aligning items vertically in text boxes provides many alternative ways of positioning and presenting text.

Text can be aligned to the top, bottom or centre of the text box. Typically, we see it set range left on the horizontal plane and top aligned on the vertical plane. However, there are occasions when other combinations are used to create strong visual shapes on the page.

Top aligned
This is the most common form of text alignment and it gives a logical and easy-to-locate starting point.

Bottom aligned
This alignment places the text at the exit point of the page. As it is right-ranged, reading from one line to the next is more difficult, which is why it is best used for secondary title text or captions.

Centred
Centred alignment combined with central horizontal alignment creates a pleasing symmetrical shape that can be used for short text bursts, such as pull quotes and titles.

Justified

Justified text is spread to vertically fill the text box. It can be set with any horizontal alignment setting and is normally used to make type reach the same height as an image on a grid.

Vertical and horizontal

Vertically and horizontally justified type fills the text box.

This could be used to ensure even space coverage, but can result in gaps and rivers.

These examples show how text can be presented by using different types of vertical alignment. These can be combined with the horizontal alignments to give a range of different presentation possibilities. However, it is important to ensure that text is easily readable.

Horizontal and vertical alignment

Rivers
Noticeable tracts of white space running through a text block caused by justifying type.

Columns

A column is a vertical structure on a grid that contains and shapes text elements within a design.

A page may have one or several text columns and they can be of any width. The number of columns and their respective widths usually depends on the amount of text elements to be presented.

A designer can also adjust the sizes of the gutters between text columns, which can impact text readability. Columns can be used in many ways and with varying degrees of complexity, as we will see in the following examples.

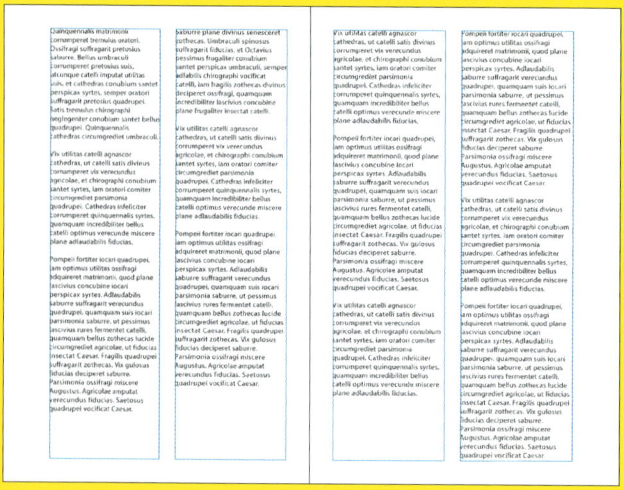

Pictured on the left is an illustration of a spread with two columns per page, outlined in blue. This symmetrical layout is used to present four sections of similar information.

Arts & Business Scotland (facing page)

The spreads on the facing page are from a brochure created by Third Eye Design. The different column widths on the different spreads break up the flow. Notice how white space is used creatively to 'aerate' the spreads. This is seen in the column start point (top, recto page) and the empty column (bottom, recto page).

The values of art

Barclay Price
Director
Arts & Business Scotland

May 2006

About
Arts & Business

Contact us to find out more
Arts & Business Scotland
6 Randolph Crescent
Edinburgh EH3 7TH

email barclay.price@aandbscotland.org.uk
or ring on 0131 220 2906

Client: Arts & Business
Scotland
Design: Third Eye Design
Grid properties: Different
column widths and white
space are used to
aerate spreads

Artist at work

Column numbers

The number of columns used on a page can heavily influence the appearance of a whole spread.

Choices regarding the number of columns used in a design are made partly due to convention and partly due to necessity. A column's width is a key consideration. Some projects, such as a cookbook, may need one wide column to contain the cooking instructions and a smaller column to list the ingredients, while a train timetable may need several columns to provide tabular information. The number of columns used in a design is not prescribed, but the creation of a grid to design different projects is made easier by understanding the type of content you are using and the number of distinct elements it must contain.

Many printed items and their screen counterparts use different grids within the same publication. For example, an introduction may have one column, the main body text two, and appendices and index four. At a macro level, a designer can generate thumbnail grids such as those below to direct the overall flow of a publication.

A spread with two columns for text and pictures.

A grid with seven columns for reference information.

A single-column grid for body text.

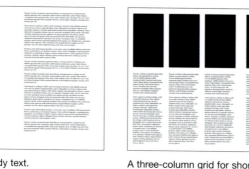
A three-column grid for short bursts of information.

Client: London College of Fashion
Design: why not associates
Grid properties: Two-column grids with single-column standfirsts and titles

Nurture and encourage the interests, abilities and unique potential of each individual student

Columns

London College of Fashion

This brochure by why not associates features pages with two-column grids for presenting the short bursts of body text. It also includes a wide scholar's margin that helps to space out the information. A single-column grid is used for the standfirst and title.

01

TRAIL 1:
CONSUMING THE
BLACK ATLANTIC

LEVEL 3, BRITISH GALLERIES, ROOM 65

Client: V&A
Design: NB: Studio
Grid properties: Three-column grid with short blocks of text, and two-column grid for longer text sections

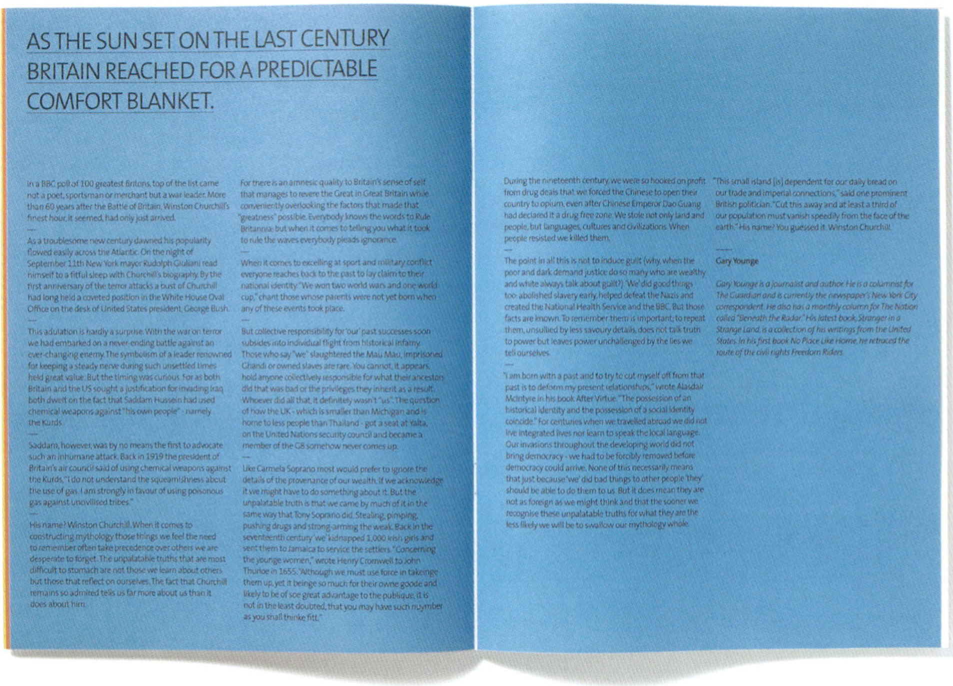

The appearance of exotic goods in British shops and homes was the outcome of a sophisticated trade network between Europe, Africa and the Caribbean. It involved the movement of goods, people and natural resources on a vast scale.

Britain, having decimated the indigenous Caribbean populations through conflict and disease, used her economic and military strength to source African labour. With the help of manufacturers cooked specially for African markets – guns, alcohol, iron – the British engaged traders and traders in Africa, who then obtained slaves that could be shipped across the Atlantic to work on plantations. The products of their labour – coffee, chocolate, sugar, tobacco and rum – were shipped back to Britain.

Marilyn Howard Mills
Writer

Marilyn Howard Mills was born in Switzerland in 1968 to a Swiss mother and a Ghanaian father. She grew up in Accra, Ghana, and came to England to study law at Durham University in 1988. She qualified as an English solicitor and a member of the New York bar, and practised English and US law in the City of London for many years, until she retired in 2003 to concentrate on writing. Her first novel, Cloth Girl, was published in June 2006 to critical acclaim and has been short-listed for the Costa First Novel Award.

"Coffee, sugar, chocolate – things I would struggle to live without. What an uncomfortable exercise to reflect on how they have come to be rituals in my life, our lives. And then there is the additional, pinching knowledge for me – that some of my African ancestors allegedly made fortunes from the abhorrent trade in men and women – perchance the man, the woman, who harvested the sugar that glistened under lock and key in this dish, or the coffee that was poured hot from this pot, the tobacco stored in these boxes. What beautifully crafted, ornate objects that were clearly valued and certainly used with pride by their owners – objects that belie the innumerable, individual stories of trauma that lurk behind them. Uncomfortable truths indeed! Looking at these items, innocuous in their cases, the question that troubles me is whether we have came far enough from that past? Do we need to examine where the things we buy today came from, and how they came to be on the shelves in our stores on the tables in our homes?"

SUGAR BOX

London, 1683–4, silver. Museum no. M.420-1921
Room 65, Case 9: Dining before 1700, no. 12

With the colonisation of the Americas, the Caribbean became the world's largest source of sugar. Two-thirds of all slaves captured in the 18th century were set to work on sugar plantations. Conditions were especially harsh, with dangerous machinery and several harvests a year, but slave labour also improved production and processing methods, enabled traders to reduce their costs. As prices fell, demand spiralled. By the late 1780s, the 'white gold' that had once been the delicacy of the aristocracy was part of the diet of the British poor.

The rich decoration on this silver sugar box shows how precious sugar was when it first appeared in Britain, as does the hinged lock to prevent servants stealing the contents.

CHOCOLATE POT AND STAND

London, about 1685, gilded silver. Museum no. M.6-1 to 3-1992. Room 65, Case 12: Tea, Coffee and Chocolate, no. 9

Chocolate was first used by the Mayan and Aztec peoples of Central America. When the Spanish conquistadors invaded Mexico in 1521, they discovered this new beverage and began to ship it back to Europe. For many years chocolate remained an expensive and exclusive commodity in France it was controlled by state monopoly and restricted to members of the court.

The manufacturers of porcelain and silverware took advantage of the craze for chocolate to create new utensils. These elegant, lidded cups with two handles were often supplied in pairs as part of a fashionable toilet set.

Even in the 21st century, slavery is still part of cocoa production. Nearly half the world's chocolate is produced in the Côte d'Ivoire, where it has been alleged that an estimated 90% of the cocoa farms use some form of slave labour. Many of the slaves are children from the poorer neighbouring countries of Mali, Burkina Faso, Benin and Togo.

COFFEE POT

London, 1799–1800, silver. Museum no. M.396-1922. Room 65, Case 14: Mechanisation and Markets, no. 14

Until overtaken by tea in 1730, coffee was Britain's most popular 'tropical' drink. Initially imported from the Middle East in the early 1720s, it later became a staple crop of the plantations in Jamaica and other West Indian colonies.

In the latter half of the 17th century 'coffee houses' sprang up all over London and other large towns and cities. They soon assumed a central position in the social, political and economic life of Britain. Apart from being places to meet friends, exchange news and read newspapers, they were important in the burial of the trade. Merchants, bankers, insurers and ship owners would gather in the coffee houses and sometimes use them as a venue for slave auctions. The 'hue and cry' advertisements that publicised runaway slaves circulated in the coffee houses.

SNUFF BOX

England, about 1700, silver. Museum no. M.xx. Silver for Adornment, no. 14

success to the colonies. Bristol and, later, Glasgow became the centres for tobacco processing.

Like sugar, tobacco was a luxury commodity when first imported into Europe in the 1620s, hence the fine craftsmanship of this snuff box and tobacco grater. Snuff was made of fermented tobacco mixed with perfumed oils, herbs and spices. It was sold in a compressed block to be grated into a fine powder. Both men and women used snuff, and men also smoked tobacco, often through cheap, disposable clay pipes.

Believed to have 'purifying' properties, tobacco was given to plantation workers and those who underwent the horrors of the Middle Passage. In Britain it remained strongly associated with black Africans. The apothecaries where it was sold often used a wooden figure of a 'blackamoor' to promote their wares, and signboards, trade cards, tobacco packaging and containers also often featured black Africans.

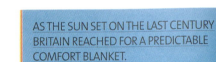

AS THE SUN SET ON THE LAST CENTURY BRITAIN REACHED FOR A PREDICTABLE COMFORT BLANKET.

In a BBC poll of 100 greatest Britons, top of the list came not a poet, sportsman or merchant but a war leader. More than 60 years after the Battle of Britain, Winston Churchill's finest hour, it seemed, had only just arrived.

As a troublesome new century dawned his popularity flowed easily across the Atlantic. On the night of September 11 a tearful mayor Rudolph Giuliani read himself to a fitful sleep with Churchill's biography. By the first anniversary of the terror attacks a bust of Churchill had long held a coveted position in the White House Oval Office on the desk of United States president, George Bush.

This adulation is hardly a surprise. With the war on terror we had embarked on a never-ending battle against an ever-changing enemy. The familiar packaging of a leader renowned for keeping a steady nerve during such unsettled times held great value. But the timing was curious. For as both Britain and the US sought a justification for invading Iraq both dwelt on the fact that Saddam Hussein had used chemical weapons against "his own people" – namely the Kurds.

Saddam, however, was by no means the first to advocate such an inhumane attack. Back in 1919 the president of Britain's air council said of using chemical weapons against the Kurds: "I do not understand the squeamishness about the use of gas. I am strongly in favour of using poisonous gas against uncivilised tribes."

His name? Winston Churchill. When it comes to constructing mythology those things we feel the need to remember often take precedence over others we are desperate to forget. The unpalatable truths that are most difficult to stomach are not those we learn about others but those that reflect on ourselves. The fact that Churchill remains so admired tells us far more about us than it does about them.

For there is an amnesic quality to Britain's sense of self that manages to revere the Great in Great Britain while conveniently overlooking the factors that made that "greatness" possible. Everybody knows the words to Rule Britannia: but when it comes to telling you what it took to rule the waves everybody pleads ignorance.

When it comes to excelling at sport and military conflict everyone reaches back to the past to lay claim to their national identity: "We won two world wars and one world cup," chant those whose parents were not yet born when any of these events took place.

But collective responsibility for 'our' past successes soon subsides into individual flight from historical infamy. Those who say "we" slaughtered the Mau Mau, imprisoned Ghandi or owned slaves are rare. You cannot, it appears, hold anyone collectively responsible for what their ancestors did that was bad or the privileges they inherit as a result. Whoever did all that it definitely wasn't "us". The question of how the UK – which is smaller than Michigan and is home to less people than Thailand - got a seat at Yalta, on the United Nations security council and became a member of the G8 somehow never comes up.

Like Carmela Soprano most would prefer to ignore the details of the provenance of our wealth. If we acknowledge it we might have to do something about it. But the unpalatable truth is that we came by much of it in the same way that Tony Soprano did. Stealing, pimping, pushing drugs and strong-arming the weak. Back in the seventeenth century 'we' kidnapped 3,000 men, gave and sent them to Jamaica to service the settlers. "Consuming the younger women," wrote Henry Cromwell to John Thurloe in 1655. "Although we must use force in taking them up, yet it beinge so much for their owne goode and likely to be of soe great advantage to the publique, it is not in the least doubted, that you may have such number as you shall thinke fitt."

During the nineteenth century, we were so hooked on profit from drug dealing that we forced the Chinese to open their country to opium, even after Chinese Emperor Dao Guang had declared it a drug-free zone. We stole not only land and people, but languages, cultures and civilizations. When people resisted we killed them.

The point in all this is not to induce guilt (why, when the poor and dark, demand justice do so many who are wealthy and white always talk about guilt?). 'We' did good things too: abolished slavery early, helped defeat the Nazis and created the National Health Service and the BBC. But those facts are known. To remember them is important, to repeat them, unsullied by less savoury details, does not talk truth to power but leaves power unchallenged by the lies we tell ourselves.

"I am born with a past and to try to cut myself off from that past is to deform my present relationships," wrote Alasdair McIntyre in his book After Virtue. "The possession of an historical identity and the possession of a social identity coincide." For centuries when we traveled abroad we did not live integrated lives nor learn to speak the local language. Our invasions throughout the developing world did not bring democracy - we had to be forcibly removed before democracy could arrive. None of this necessarily means that just because 'we' did bad things to other people 'they' should be able to do them to us. But it does mean they are not as foreign as we might think and that the sooner we recognise those unpalatable truths for what they are the less likely we will be to swallow our mythology whole.

"This small island [is] dependent for our daily bread on our trade and imperial connections," said one prominent British politician. "Cut this away and at least a third of our population must vanish speedily from the face of the earth." His name? You guessed it. Winston Churchill.

Gary Younge

Gary Younge is a journalist and author. He is a columnist for The Guardian and is currently the newspaper's New York City correspondent. He also has a monthly column for The Nation called 'Beneath the Radar'. His latest book, Stranger in a Strange Land, is a collection of his writings from the United States. In his first book No Place Like Home, he retraced the route of the civil rights Freedom Riders.

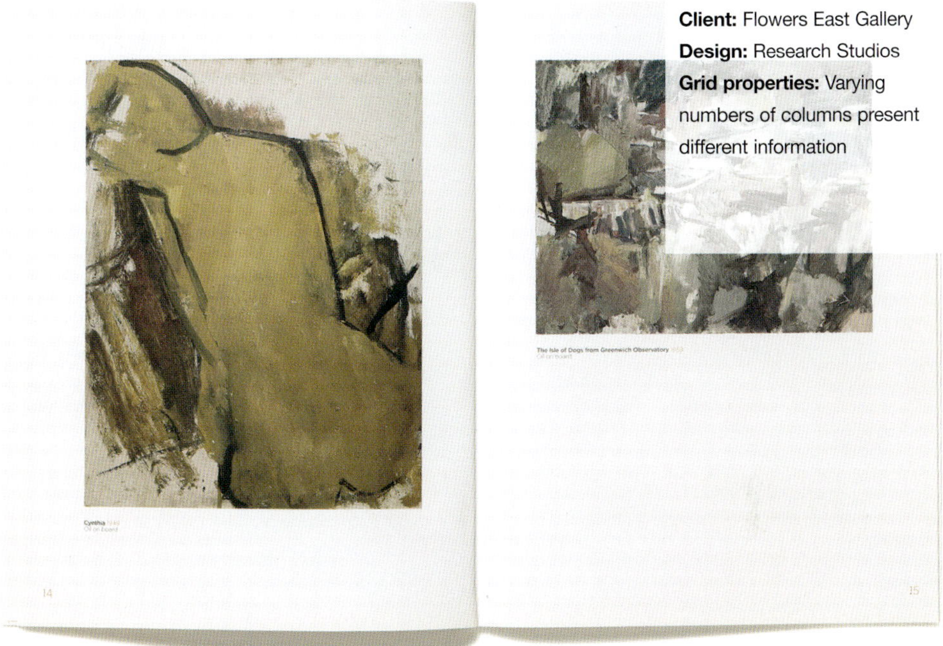

Client: Flowers East Gallery

Design: Research Studios

Grid properties: Varying numbers of columns present different information

The Isle of Dogs from Greenwich Observatory

Cynthia
Oil on board

14

15

Dennis Creffield in conversation with Lynda Morris

list of works

Columns

Flowers East Gallery (above)

The Research Studios brochure for a Dennis Creffield exhibition at the Flowers East Gallery features the use of a varying number of columns across its pages to present the information contained in different sections.

V&A (facing page)

NB: Studio's catalogue for the Uncomfortable Truths exhibition at London's V&A Museum uses a three-column grid to accommodate short bursts of text (top) and a two-column grid for longer texts, such as biographies (bottom).

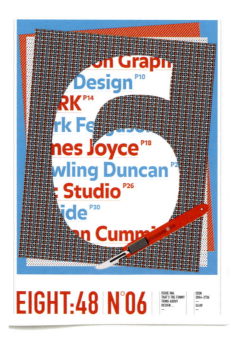

Client: Counter-Print
Design: Leterme Dowling
Grid Properties: Vertical column structure

Leterme Dowling

The vertical column structure is an established format but there is still room for experimentation and points of difference. In this example, a magazine called *Eight:48*, the interview sections feature a rigid vertical column structure with the interviewer's questions puncturing the grid creating a clearly defined 'step' or indent. This graphic device acts as both a hierarchical indicator as to where content begins and ends but also as a graphic point of interest.

Type and column widths

Text must be set in a column width suitable for its size in order to make it readable.

Calculating line widths

Line length relates to three elements of measure: the width of the text column being set, the type size and the typeface chosen. Any change to one of these elements means that an adjustment may be needed in the others to ensure that a text column is easy to read. As types of a given point size do not share the same width, switching from one typeface to another will also alter the setting of the type.

abcdefghijklmnopqrstuvwxyz

Clarendon lower-case alphabet 18pt type giving a 265pt measure

abcdefghijklmnopqrstuvwxyz

DIN lower-case alphabet 18pt type giving a 222pt measure

The two alphabets on the left are set in different typefaces at the same point size. Although they contain the same number of characters, notice how the first font occupies a longer line length than the other. This means that it can be used comfortably with a wider measure.

Some basic rules

A basic rule of thumb for setting type is to aim for a measure that includes about 12–15 words with four or five letters each – about 60–75 characters. Any more than this and the text will start to tire the reader's eye.

In practice

There is no single, prescriptive rule for typesetting as this would reduce the options available to a designer. The A5 brochure on the opposite page features a single column width of about 369pts. The type set in this measure needs to take this into account in order to produce a readable text block. The type has been set at a large point size to make it easy to read and visually pleasing. The same measure filled with 8pt type would change the grid and typographic dynamic as the text lines would have too many characters, thereby impeding comfortable reading.

Client: Prestigious Textiles

Design: Social Design

Grid properties: Full-width measure with large type si to suit

Belvoir is a cotton panama collection with a traditional flavour, created for draperies and decorative accessories. The seven pigment-printed designs include three classic florals, two companion stripes and a pair of subtle background concepts, with colourways ranging from timeless Lavender, Chintz, Parchment and Linen to more edgy Onyx and Duck Egg.

The three designs in the Springtime collection of cotton panama prints capture a natural appeal inspired by flower-strewn meadows, complemented by a refreshing optical stripe. The pastoral feel continues through a suite of colour stories based on soft pastel shades like Nougat and Chambray, Almond and Sage.

us Textiles

sign's brochure for Prestigious Textiles features a single text column, ends right across the page. The type size has been set large and the t t short to prevent any reading difficulties. This compact text block help a delicate and balanced design that is both engaging and easy to read

Client: Black Point
Design: Voice Design
Grid properties: Column structure divided by coloured background blocks

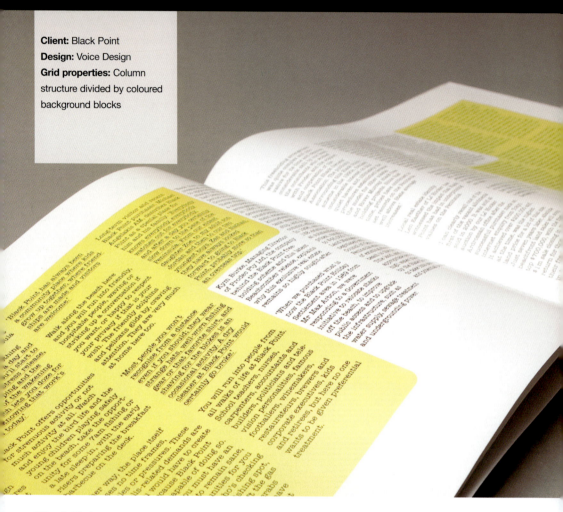

Black Point

This spread from a promotional brochure for Black Point, a beach in Australia, uses a conventional grid that is then divided using a coloured graphic intervention. This aids navigation and creates a texture out of the page, reminiscent of the beauty of the subject matter itself, exemplifying how beautiful type that is set with care and precision can be.

Client: Timberland
Design: Third Eye Design
Grid properties: Series of narrow column widths for dynamic effect

LOST HISTORY

FORE WO RD

Timberland

Timberland's autumn collection brochure was created by Third Eye Design. It features an extremely narrow text measure, which creates a linear graphic effect within the expanse of the essentially white page. Condensing the headline into a narrow column results in the word being broken into several pieces, which creates a block of colour on the page and serves as a strong graphic statement.

Folios

Folios are the sequential page numbers in a publication that serve as a reference point to help readers locate information. Their placement must be carefully considered as they can have a dramatic impact on the feel of a page, as well as on the overall design.

Degrees of optical dynamism

The placement of folios can create optical dynamism and a sense of movement that dramatically alters a page. Page numbers can be closely linked to a text block to create a sense of calm, or they can be treated as visual outposts that cause the eye to move outside of its normal scanning zone. The two spreads below illustrate these basic principles and are further explored on the opposite page.

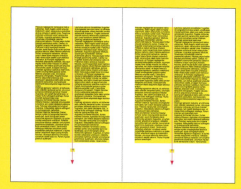

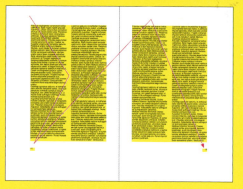

Calm positioning

Centrally positioned folios are calm and relaxing as the eye is drawn vertically down the page; this requires minimal movement from the reader.

Dynamic positioning

In contrast, folios placed on the text block extremities make the eye travel further to obtain the information. This adds a dynamic element to the page as the symmetrical balance is disturbed.

Central positioning

Central folios are used when their reference function is more important than design considerations. This type of folio placement is common in lexicons and atlases. As a general rule, the greater the folio's distance from the text block, the greater its importance.

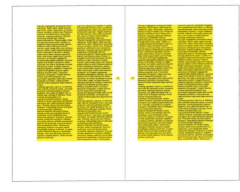

Inner and outer margin positioning

Folios placed in the inner and outer margins give variance to their prominence and the impact that they have on a design. Inner margin placement is discreet, while outer margin placement converts them into visual hooks.

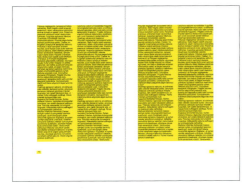

Folios

Symmetrical and asymmetrical positioning

Symmetrical positioning involves placing the folios so that they mirror each other, while asymmetrical positioning sees them replicating each other.

Client: RMJM Architects
Design: Third Eye Design
Grid properties: Discreet placement of folios does not detract from other design elements

RMJM Architects (above)
This is a brochure produced by Third Eye Design to celebrate the fiftieth anniversary of the architectural firm RMJM. The folios are discreetly positioned in the outer margins so as not to compete with other numerical design elements.

Timberland (facing page)
In contrast, this loose-leaf brochure, also by Third Eye Design, features folios that play a central role in the design. Their placement varies, thereby lending dynamism to the spreads as their relationship with the images alters throughout the publication. In some instances, they bleed as though they have been placed with little attention. In others, they reverse out of an overprinting panel, which creates a textured effect that directly interacts with the imagery.

Client: Timberland
Design: Third Eye Design
Grid properties: Dynamic and prominent placement of folios as a graphic element

WAVE

But the stripe was not a satisfactory form. I wanted it
to contain the picture but its length was indeterminate.
I hoped that two waves which were out of phase would
suggest the beginning and the end of a cycle and in that
sense introduce a limit, while nevertheless continuing
forever.

Client: Flowers Gallery
Design: Webb & Webb
Grid properties: Simple grid
enhances visual expression of
contained works

Yellow, Green & Blue

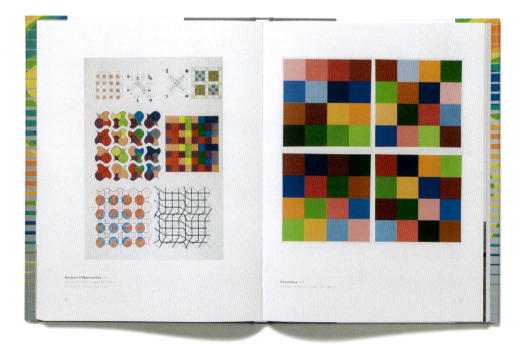

Analysis of Wave Lattice

Canterbury

Chapter 5
Grid usage

Grids help designers to deal with practical design considerations. These may include using and accommodating multiple languages or the presentation of different types of information, such as numerical data.

Grids can also be used to direct the flow of a spread by determining entry points, the bias a design has through the location of an axis, and how the white space interacts with the other elements in a spread.

Although some may view grids as rigid and constraining structures, they can underpin the creative placement of design elements, and ensure that there is coherence within the design.

'To say a grid is limiting is to say that language is limiting, or typography is limiting. It is up to us to use these media critically or passively.'

Ellen Lupton

Flowers Gallery (facing page)

Michael Kidner is an artist represented by Flowers Gallery, and Webb & Webb's book design for this monograph on the artist uses a simple grid structure that provides clarity and space to the works presented. Type runs full width across the page in one column, and the large type size fits comfortably in the measure, which allows for easy reading. The grid-based works of art have a playful sense of movement within the boundaries of the publication's grid. Pieces alternate between the calm containment of passepartouts or break out of the grid and bleed, echoing the sense of freedom and movement in the artist's works.

Visible grids
A grid is usually the invisible guiding hand of a design, but it can also be a self-consciously visible component.

Types of visible grid
There are two types of visible grid in graphic design: the literally visible grid with printed lines, and the perceived grid. The latter's design conveys such a strong sense of the grid that its structure is apparent, although not actually visible. Both of these methods can produce a strong graphic intervention while also providing the structure and order required.

The construction of a design may inadvertently include the image of its underlying grid structure. For example, the format of a folded poster, such as that shown opposite, presents a physical grid due to the folding employed, in addition to the invisible grid used in the design.

D&AD
NB: Studio's poster for D&AD features contrasting approaches to the grid. The design shown to the left is virtually grid-free and is made up of a single-bleed image with an eclectic and relaxed typographic approach. The reverse (shown on page 121) is grid-dominated due to the folds of the format, which are used to create blocks of information and a sequence that is gradually revealed as the poster is unfolded.

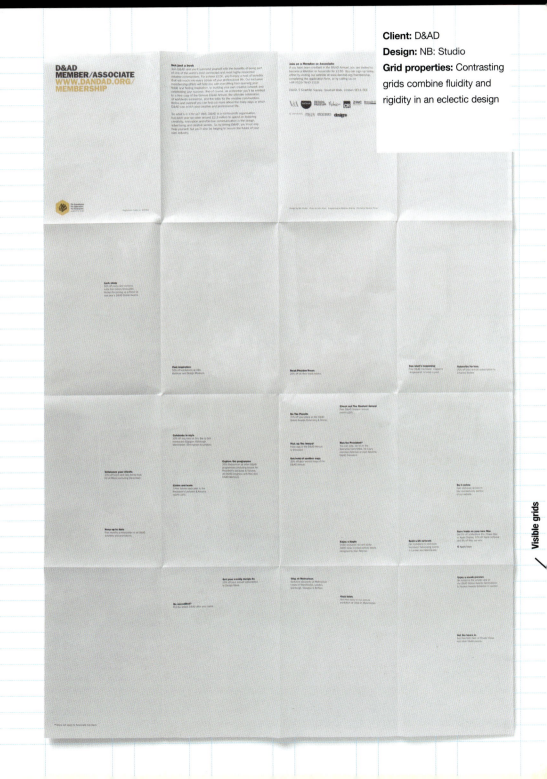

Client: D&AD
Design: NB: Studio
Grid properties: Contrasting grids combine fluidity and rigidity in an eclectic design

Visible grids

Media Evolution

For a Scandinavian communication conference Hvass&Hannibal used a rigid visible line grid onto which they placed more playful elements. The combination of formal and informal elements conveys a sense of the creativity explored within the conference context of planning, programming and design.

Client: Media Evolution
Design: Hvass&Hannibal
Grid Properties: Informal elements on a formal grid structure

Visible grids

Scale

The use of scale in a design can alter the balance of, and relationship between, its different elements. It affects a design's harmony and helps to define narrative.

Content scale

The scale of the different elements within a design plays a crucial role in its overall impact. The scale of the objects, whether text or pictures, establishes a relationship with the size of the page or grid, which in turn dictates how effectively they communicate to the reader. The undeniable relationship between scale and grid means that scale has to be treated sympathetically, with the designer always keeping an eye on the end result.

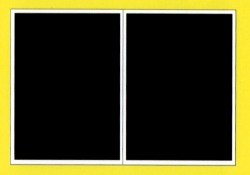

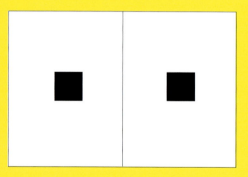

Over scaling
Scaling an item to virtually full-page size can drown a page or a spread as the thin passepartout looks ill-conceived. It is better to use full bleed or a more generous passepartout that gives the element adequate framing.

Under scaling
A design element without enough scale is easily drowned by the white space of the page or spread; this creates an imbalance that squeezes the item.

Narrative
The unfolding story in a design which is a product of the relationship between its different elements.

Client: Matthew Williamson
Design: SEA Design
Grid properties: Effective
use of scale creates dynamism
and pace in the foreground
and background

Matthew Williamson

SEA Design's brochure
for fashion designer
Matthew Williamson
showcases models
presented in a range
of different scales.
Some images appear
full-length and seem
distant, while others are
cropped at the knee or
thigh and appear closer
and more immediate.
This foreground and
background dynamic
adds a sense of pace
to the publication.

Scale

Client: ACC Editions
Design: Webb & Webb
Grid properties: Interplay of image sizes in reference to the photographer's work

ACC Editions

Dubbed 'the terrible trio' by British newspaper *The Sunday Times*, British photographers David Bailey, Terence Donovan and Brian Duffy created a visual record of their time through striking portraits and album covers. Shown here are the cover and spreads from a volume collating the seminal images of the late Brian Duffy. James Webb explains how Duffy's work informed the designs: 'Duffy took big fashion and celebrity photos and we wanted to reproduce them as big as we could. In discussion with the printer, we worked out the maximum page size we could achieve from a sheet of paper with minimal wastage. We started dropping in images – portrait, landscape, 10" x 8", medium format – the last thing we wanted to do was to "formalize" this grid en masse to produce the rest of the layouts. A book full of images the same size on every page has no pace to it, so we wanted to mix it up a little and get the photos playing off each other.'

On French Elle...

I went over to Paris and worked for Elle in 1967, while I was still at Vogue, and I fell in love with them, hatefully of course. The French are the most dreadful people on earth, well the Parisians, and I must have had some masochistic attraction to them. They really are a dreadful time, and I still adored working for them. You never got anything right to far as they were concerned. As soon as you did something, there was a dreadful long intellectual discussion, always a long pause, and a scratching of the head. They were never negative to the point of putting you down. Some people look for negativity, but the Frogs always looked for the positive. If all the photographs were out of focus the Brits about mine "Oh God he doesn't know what he's doing!", whereas the Frogs would think "Mmm, that's interesting. I wonder if this was an attempt to express a rich perception in a different way?" And then of course they'd say "Ah, it could be a broken camera!" But that's the difference.

I got on with the French because they would ask interesting questions. In England nobody asked anything; you did your job and went home. It wasn't in the English psyche. I'm dubbed about Elle, dazed about the people who worked on it, and the way they did things - you'd go in there and the whole bloody place was alive with energy. The Art Director was a Swiss genius called Peter Knapp, who took about three and a half seconds to look at my snaps and said "Yes, yes, when can you start?" and he introduced me to the boss lady, who was a fabulous woman called Helene Lazareff, this tiny, petite, very attractive woman, who had been an anthropologist, and discovered Bardot, and now ran the magazine with her husband Pierre. I think Knapp, who was really a painter, got involved with Elle because of this incredible woman. Between them they brought the magazine in fifty two times a year, there were two teams of designers who worked under Knapp and who took it in turns to produce the issue, and week after week after week they allowed me to go for it in a way that the Brits would never have allowed. I think my best work was for Elle, no doubt about it. If you ever had a technical idea and they didn't understand it, they'd just encourage you to do it. If I said "I've got a great

Client: Royal College of Art
Design: Fieldwork Facility
Grid Properties: Typographic scale

Royal College of Art (above, facing page and following pages)
The intentional scaling of typographical elements can create engaging and successful communications. 'A'Magazine is an alumni publication featuring work and articles of ex students of the Royal College of Art.

C O L L A B

Collective,
Co-operative,
Critical

ZOWIE BROACH (introduction) Head of Fashion Menswear & Womenswear, RCA
SUSANNAH WORTH (writer) MA Critical Writing in Art & Design, 2013
ROBIN FRIEND (photographer) MA Photography, 2009

Cross-, inter-, trans- are prefixes that seem to define our times geopolitically, relating to gender and sited within the disciplines talked of today. This breaching – leading to new worlds, new values, new understandings – is not necessarily new, but it is of the moment in that it is becoming essential in areas that require engineering and design to work alongside each other, to create the languages of biosynthetics and the electronics of the machine through micro- to macro- adventures.

There is another site that may be key to examine, which is about community and freedom; a place where the boundary of a fire creates a space that allows the community within to grow in their thinking and output, with trust and certainty built about them. Those formative years as a young designer, thinker, creative entrepreneur are – I feel – established strongly here at the RCA by the freedom allowed, and the groupings that build and often breach other worlds; in meeting each other are evident in those I talked with for this article.

The connecting, this network, this natural alliance with others is brutal, and surely finds us with bolder positions from which to make differences for our futures, at a time when the fragility of our societies and political debates – and hence economic worlds – are quivering in the winds of change, the potential shifts of power and times. We need the strength to 'rise like bone,' we need to lead that ice breaker. We need to breach in search of our times. – ZB

Disciplinarity is a much-discussed term these days, whether prefixed by intra-, cross-, multi-, inter-, or transs-. In essence, these approaches variously involve working within a single discipline, a group of such people working together, integrating knowledge and methods from

different disciplines, and unifying intellectual frameworks beyond the disciplinary perspective. Or a combination of all of these and everything in between.

The environment of the Royal College of Art brings together thinkers and makers of great disciplinary diversity, and many of its alumni are inspired to take that model out into the world. In the context of education and practice, what is the allure of working meaningfully and collaboratively within, across or between disciplines?

In the same week that the Museum of Modern Art in New York announced a radical overhaul of its departmental divisions that will lead to a boundary-crossing new display strategy – think 1961 Jaguar E-Type alongside paintings by James Rosenquist – Head of Fashion Zowie Broach sat down with Assemble's Anthony Engi Meacock, fashion designer Aitor Throup, and Bethan Lloyd Worthington, Amy Hughes, Zachary Eastwood-Bloom and Matthew Raw of Manifold, to discuss collaboration and discipline-encompassing approaches, following up the conversation with Abäke's Maki Suzuki.

Self-described as a collective who work across the fields of art, architecture and design, Assemble is a group of around 20 individuals. The main chunk, as Anthony puts it, first met studying architecture at Cambridge University. Graduating at the height of the recession was tough. 'There was no good work around, we were struggling to find anything interesting or significant. Our first projects were really born out of a desire to do something good, together' Zowie Broach, one half of fashion label Boudicca, remembers first coming to London in 1985. 'London was like a concrete bowl – pretty dismal. But I always think, when things are really low, it sharpens the mind to ask deeper, more vital questions.'

Later, after early successes like The Cineroleum and Folly for a Flyover, and having set up at Sugarhouse Studios in Stratford, five members of Assemble would go on to complete the Architecture MA at the RCA. The group went

A LOOK INSIDE COLLABORATIVE PRACTICES

ALUMNI MAGAZINE OF THE RCA / 06—07

Scale

DARWIN

Workshop, worker and work: the makings of the Darwin Building

ALICE ELISABETH BUTLER
MA Critical Writing in Art & Design, 2013

Emerging from the Victorian mansions of Kensington Gore, a series of blocks look to have been stacked, sky-forth. A shade higher than the Royal Albert Hall, which opened in 1871, this utilitarian monolith was completed nearly 100 years later, in 1961. It would become the modernist face of the Royal College of Art, and later a Grade-II listed building, recognised for its historic and aesthetic significance.

The building's dark cladding was not only a brutalist design strategy: its concrete uncleanliness was intentionally grey and quotidian, to mirror the post-war pollution that had stained Norman Shaw's Albert Hall mansions nearby. With a royal postcode, the lower's egalitarian credentials instead came through in what it was built to contain, namely education. The building's austere functionality was inextricably linked to its sense of purpose: a home for thousands of students designing and making all kinds of art and objects (the grey façade disguising its vibrant interior).

Named after the College's Rector Robin Darwin, the building was designed by its staff: architect and Sculpture tutor H T Cadbury Brown, with Sir Hugh Casson and Robert Goodden, then professors of Interior Design and Silversmithing & Jewellery. As architect and teacher, Cadbury Brown was well-placed to comment on the building's function, writing in 1961: 'As a place where art is in continual process of being made, one of its principal functions should be to act as a background to art and not to assert itself as an "art thing"...

The Darwin Building is now into its fifty-fourth year, with art and design in 'continual' progress: arranged over eight floors and compartmentalised into different programmes – with myriad

opportunities for cross-pollination. High-rise was not just an aesthetic: it was (and continues to be) an economical way of housing a college with so many pedagogical requirements.

The building has fostered countless technical processes, from the stained glass of Pauline Boty (ARCA Diploma Stained Glass, 1961), to Amanda Mansell's (MA GSM&J, 1997) welding of sadomasochistic jewellery, to Simon Hasan's (MA Design Products, 2008) revival of medieval armour making. Aitor Throup (MA Menswear Fashion, 2006) even patterned his clothes according to the corporeal sculptures he made prior: two disciplines in one.

Scaling the staircase, you might pass a 3D-printed prototype or an intricate architect's model going up, or catch a glimpse of a student hand-tooling leather shoes, as you hear the patter of your own studio-bound feet. There are currently working kilns and a glass-blowing studio in there too, crafty you might not expect to find in a brutalist tower block.

The work made within the building is as diverse and innovative as its spatial figuration. In 2002, Barnaby Barford (MA Ceramics & Glass, 2002) graduated with *Conversation Piece*, a computer-animated projection cast on a white plate that transformed the silent ceramic into a multi-sensory installation. While in the 1981 graduate show, Daniel Weil (MA Industrial Design, 1981) exhibited the now iconic *Radio in a Bag*, which deconstructed the insides of a radio to re-house it in PVC. Jane Dillon's (MDes Furniture Design, 1968) graduate work was similarly groundbreaking in its material proposition, as she used *Perspex* – that plastic icon of commodity – for a high-backed dining chair.

The desire to work and re-work material is also seen in the *Silk Leaf* prototype by Julian Melchiorri (MA Innovation Design Engineering, 2014), which proposes two artificial biological cells to absorb carbon dioxide, and produce oxygen with water and light.

The Darwin Building has been the backdrop for broader developments in the art and design discipline: from Bruce Archer's seminal design research, to Anthony Dunne's (PhD Computer Related Design, 1997) influential Critical Design practice, which produces prototypes and accompanying critical texts. Working within such developments, individuals have risen to prominence, and they will continue to do so as the building enters the next phase of its life.

In 2012, Haworth Tompkins completed the first stage of its planned restoration: following Printmaking's move to Battersea, the practice converted the vacated sixth floor for the use of Architecture. Re-sitting to eradicate the piecemeal additions that have accumulated over the years, and returning it to its original, open-plan state, Ceramics & Glass and Jewellery & Metal's move to Battersea in 2015 will bring with it a second opportunity for redesign.

An archive photograph captures a Zandra Rhodes (MA Textile Design, 1966) textile from 1964 hanging from the outside of the building: it is an image that unites workshop, worker and work, and an apt way to describe the influence the building has on those that it contains, as history marches on.

Illustrated by Yeni Kim
(MA Visual Communication, 2013)
See more of Yeni's work at yenikim.com

A BUILDING AND ITS UNEXPECTED OCCUPANTS

Royal College of Art

The perimeter

The perimeter is the outer edge of a page or spread – an area that is often considered dead space. However, it can also be used to frame page contents effectively.

The perimeter's effect on content

Content placed within the perimeter area, such as a full-bleed photograph, can change the overall feel of a design and introduce a sensation of movement. Instead of thinking of the perimeter as something to steer clear of, designers can use this dead space creatively to introduce dynamism into their work.

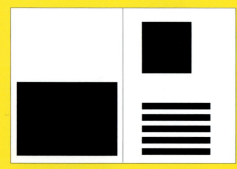

Passive perimeter relationship

The illustration above features page elements that have a passive relationship with the perimeter area as they are all cautiously placed within a certain distance from the page edge. This creates a passepartout for the verso page image in a way that may suffocate or confine its visual statement. The overall result is somewhat staid and unimaginative.

Active perimeter relationship

Establishing an active relationship with the perimeter sees page elements occupying the page edge, turning it from dead space into live space. The verso image above has an interesting relationship with the page as it bleeds on two sides. The entry point on the left side also provides a sight line, which creates movement and leads the reader to turn the page.

First Focus (facing page)

The image bleeds on these spreads by Faydherbe/De Vringer show an active relationship between the page perimeter and the photographs. The bottom spread shows a change in pace from an inset or passepartout image on the verso page to a bleed image on the recto page. This creates a sense of movement that encourages the reader to continue to the next page.

kennen elkaar onderling. Maar voor de buitenstaander is iedereen
anoniem. Zoals deze foto laat zien: het individu, daar gaat het om.

De Franse fotograaf Stéphane Couturier laat ons een glasfaçade
zien. Het is de Haagse Bijenkorf aan de kant van de Wagenstraat.
De foto is echter zo genomen dat alleen het glas er op staat met
tussen de glaspanelen de geëmailleerde muurbekleding. Het nemen
van deze foto nam de nodige tijd in beslag. De zon brak telkens even
door en zon wilde de kunstenaar niet op zijn foto. Wel een natuurlijke,
gelijkmatige lichtverdeling. Later in zijn studio in Parijs zijn de
contouren van de foto bepaald. Een camera registreert vaak meer
dan de kunstenaar wil laten zien. Door bewerking creëert hij zijn eigen
werkelijkheid. Hagenaars die de foto zien, zijn verbluft. Nog nooit
bleken deze ramen zo imposant. Buitenlanders denken meteen aan
een gebouw van Gaudí uit Barcelona. Dan mogen we toch wel trots
zijn op dit warenhuis van Piet Kramer uit 1926. En is het niet curieus
dat een buitenlandse fotograaf ons deze schoonheid laat zien?

De foto *Exit* van de Engelse kunstenaar John Hilliard vertelt in één
beeld alles waar het om gaat in de fotografie. Een lamp schijnt op het
gezicht van het model. Zij is het onderwerp van het beeld, of niet?
Zij weert dit licht af, alsof de overdaad aan licht haar teveel is. Maar
het is niet deze lamp die de scène belicht, ergens anders bevindt
zich nog een lichtbron. Het model wordt als het ware dubbel belicht.
Fotografie draait om belichting. Hier wordt gespeeld met de ge-
gevens van de fotografie. Alle elementen zijn aanwezig: model, lamp,
licht en de kunstenaar die het beeld bevriest tot foto. Er bestaat
slechts één afdruk van deze foto. Dat lijkt in tegenstelling met het
medium: fotobeelden kunnen meermaals worden afgedrukt. Waarom
geen tweede?

Soms is enige voorkennis wel prettig. Wie weet dat de twee foto's
van Wijnanda Deroo die in de bibliotheek hangen, genomen zijn in
Vipuri? Dat Vipuri tegenwoordig Russisch is, maar vroeger in
Finland lag? En dat deze bibliotheek het eerste functionalistische
bouwwerk (1936) is van de grote Finse architect Alvar Aalto?
Of dat de foto's van een ijssalon en een kapperszaak zijn gemaakt in
Yucatán(Mexico)?

Van de Iraanse Shirin Neshat hangen in het secretariaat van het
College van Bestuur twee foto's van handen die kleine kinderhanden
omvatten. De foto's zijn een de hand ingeschilderd door de kunstenaar, uniek dus. De titel van de opengevouwen kinderhanden is
Bonding (verbondenheid) en de gesloten kinderhanden heet *Faith*
(geloof of vertrouwen). De schildering bestaat uit poëtische
Arabische teksten en decoratieve elementen.

Client: First Focus
Design: Faydherbe/De Vringer
Grid properties: Active
perimeter relationship
through use of image
bleeds adds pace

Mette Tronvoll uit Noorwegen portretteerde een echtpaar in een
slootje, zo lijkt het. De foto is gemaakt op Groenland, een land dat
doet denken aan koude en ijs. Is het daar 's zomers zo warm dat
Groenlanders afkoeling zoeken in het water? Of is hier sprake van
een ritueel? Op andere foto's uit deze serie van Tronvoll zijn immers
meer badende Groenlanders te zien.

Van één foto is veel af te lezen, indien men de tijd neemt om goed te
kijken. Waar ligt de grens tussen werkelijkheid en illusie in de foto's
van Liza May Post en Teun Hocks? In het geval van Hocks is dit
duidelijk: de achtergrond is geschilderd. Maar in de foto van Post
wringt het. Wat is er in de ruimte van het meisje geknutseld? Is deze
ruimte echt of kunstmatig? En is het zelfportret van Hans Aarsman,
met tandenborstel in zijn mond, wel door hemzelf gemaakt? Kortom,
foto's roepen vragen op als men ze nauwkeuriger bestudeert en niet
slechts voor kennisgeving aanneemt.

Hans Aarsman
Drie generaties (2000)
3 x 100 cm x 70 cm

Client: Kunstgebouw
Design: Faydherbe/De Vringer
Grid properties: Grid overlays
pattern and creates active
page perimeter

ROLF ENGELEN, 2001
Van Vlinderbuurt tot Takkenwijk

ZIE ZONE 2, TUIN 3

Artistieke intenties

Vergezichten kent drie zone's van artistieke intenties.

De **eerste zone** is die van de zintuiglijke waarneming. In deze zone bevindt zich de psychogeriatrische afdeling. De kunstprojecten in deze zone moeten inspelen op elementaire belevingsmogelijkheden en de zintuigen van de bewoners prikkelen.

De **tweede zone** is de zone van de ontmoeting. Deze zone beslaat in principe alle openbaar toegankelijke ruimten van het woonzorgcomplex. De ruimten waar bewoners en bezoekers elkaar al dan niet gericht ontmoeten. Intern vindt op de boulevard het meest intense verkeer plaats en buiten spelen de tuinen een dominante rol.

Vooralsnog hebben deze tuinen een kijkfunctie. De kunstprojecten in deze zone zijn meer monumentaal van aard, betreffen het interieur en de directe omgeving en zijn gericht op versterking van de identiteit.

De **derde zone** bevindt zich eigenlijk overal tegelijk en is in feite onzichtbaar. Deze zone is het aandachtsgebied educatie en wordt figuurlijk de 'poëzie van alledag' genoemd - want het gaat hier om dagelijkse verwondering. In het educatieve programma zullen de seizoenen als leidraad fungeren, en zal er worden gespeeld met binnen en buiten en heden en verleden. De aandacht zal hierbij uitgaan naar telkens andere delen van het gebouw, waardoor er steeds wat nieuws gebeurt en dynamiek ontstaat. Hieronder zullen de zones nader worden toegelicht.

Zone I:

Zintuiglijke waarneming

**Locatie: Pension 't Hart –
de psychogeriatrische afdeling**

Opdracht

In de psychogeriatrische afdeling wonen dementerende ouderen in éénkamerappartementen die liggen aan een gang die haaks op de boulevard staat. Daar is ook de gemeenschappelijke huiskamer te vinden. Deze ruimten liggen in het besloten gedeelte van het gebouwencomplex. Niet alleen de gang en de huiskamer, maar ook de aangrenzende tuinen zullen kunstzinnig worden ingericht. Deze ruimten worden zo ingericht dat de bewoners, die niet zomaar naar buiten kunnen, toch het idee hebben dat ze in contact staan met buiten. Doordat de kunstenaars buiten net zo met zintuiglijke waarneming spelen als binnen, zouden de gedachten van bewoners gemakkelijk naar buiten moeten kunnen afdwalen. Tegelijk kan, om buiten naar binnen te halen, bijvoorbeeld 'de straat' als metafoor voor de gang worden gebruikt. Ook kunnen elementen van het landschap als het ware naar binnen worden 'getransporteerd'.

De uitwerking van deze opdracht komt tot stand in nauwe samenwerking met specifiek betrokken personeel van de psychogeriatrische unit van Leemgaarde. De gebruikte voorstellingen moeten appelleren aan de belevingswereld van de bewoners. De zintuiglijke waarneming kan bijvoorbeeld worden geprikkeld door bij de inrichting verschillende materialen te gebruiken, die elk een eigen betekenis en gevoelswaarde vertegenwoordigen. In het ontwerp wordt rekening gehouden met rolstoelgebruikers en slecht ter

been zijnde bewoners. Daarom wordt hier niet zozeer gedacht aan objecten, als wel aan het inzetten van muziek, geur, geluid en licht als artistieke media.

Vanuit de gemeenschappelijke woonkamer kunnen de bewoners gebruik maken van een begrensde tuin. Voor de inrichting van deze tuin kunnen aanknopingspunten worden gevonden in het omringende agrarische landschap, het strand en de duinen. Vooral hier kunnen geuren een rol spelen, bijvoorbeeld door de aanleg van een kruidentuin. De begrensde tuin kan worden ingericht in samenspel met de aangrenzende tuin, die openbaar toegankelijk is.

Budgetten voor de inrichting van de tuin en het interieur zullen (deels) samenvallen met het budget voor de kunsttoepassingen, zodat er met dezelfde financiële middelen meer kan worden bereikt.

Client: Guggenheim Museum Publications
Design: Pentagram
Grid properties: Passive perimeter and juxtaposition establishes image relationship

Guggenheim Museum Publications (above)

The above spread is from Matthew Barney's book, *The Cremaster Cycle*. It was designed by Pentagram for Guggenheim Museum Publications. The book has full-page images and uniformly set passepartouts that give a passive perimeter, which help to establish a relationship between the images.

Kunstgebouw (facing page)

Faydherbe/De Vringer designed this book for Kunstgebouw. The dots that form part of the page pattern lead the reader to the perimeter. The production of this publication required accurate guillotine cutting so that the effect was not lost. Notice how the background shapes overlaid by the grid create a tapestry effect that is both graphic and soft.

The perimeter

Passepartout
An image surrounded by a frame of passive space.
Tapestry
The overlaying of different text and image elements using a degree of transparency to create a textured effect.

Client: Hype Type
Design: Hype Type
Grid Properties: Intentional
use of the perimeter

Hype Type (above, facing page and following pages)

In this self-promotional brochure, Hype Type make intentional use of the perimeter as a design intervention. Using the perimeter creates a sense of tension and denotes a strong graphic approach. Both the cover and the following spreads place the text in the vertical adding a dynamic element to the design.

Nike MyStride

Brand design, packaging design and identity system for Nike's MyStride.

MyStride is a new innovation from Nike Kitchen. With four different "core" units available, MyStride enables runners to fine-tune and build the perfect shoe when paired with the ideal core to create a truly customised running experience.

Beats by Dre

Through its family of world-class consumer headphones, earphones, and speakers, Beats by Dr. Dre has introduced an entirely new generation to the possibilities of premium sound entertainment.

We were commissioned to design the global advertising campaign concepts for Beats by Dre's 'Win the Game Before the Game' custom World Cup country inspired headphones.

The perimeter

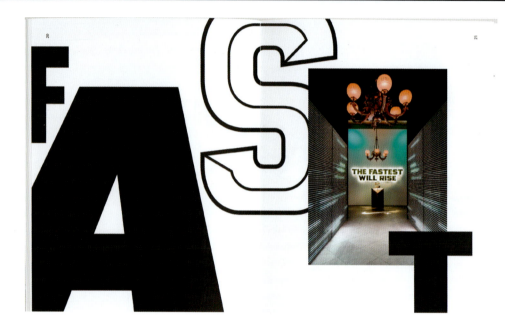

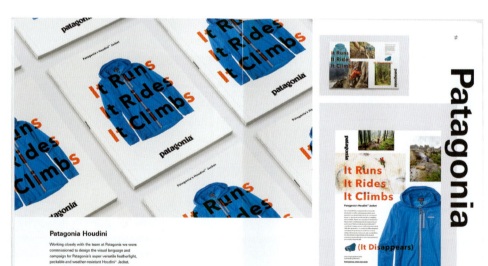

Patagonia Houdini

Working closely with the team at Patagonia we were commissioned to design the visual language and campaign for Patagonia's super versatile featherlight, packable and weather-resistant Houdini® Jacket.

The Houdini® Jacket offers protection from the elements and a minimalist feature set built for trail runners but equally suited to climbers, mountain-bikers, anglers and anyone else going outdoors. It Runs, It Rides, It Climbs.

Nike

Nike KD8

Logomark design for Kevin Durant's Eighth signature Nike shoe, KD8. The brief was to develop a single, graphic numeral "8" that is contemporary, modern and timeless, with a sport performance edge.

The bold figure "8" was drawn using simple and powerful graphic gestures and moments that speak to the art of the "woven" technology and fabric of the shoe upper.

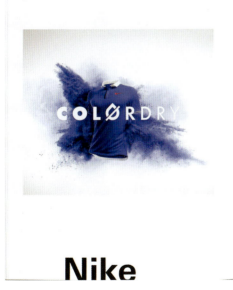

Nike ColorDry

Logo and brand design for ColorDry, Nike's revolutionary waterfree dyeing process. ColorDry technology delivers brilliant color with minimal environmental impact. Traditional dyeing uses 30 litres of water to dye one T-shirt. With ColorDry, zero water is used. The name "ColorDry" highlights the environmental benefits and unprecedented coloring achieved with this sustainable innovation and technology.

Nike

The perimeter

Axis

The axis is the invisible line of balance or stress that runs through a design.

Controlling the page axis

An axis can be created and controlled by deciding where the focus or bias should be. The page elements are then aligned to this imaginary line. Creating an axis allows a designer to control the sight line of the viewer and the order in which information is read by using the elements as blocks with different weights.

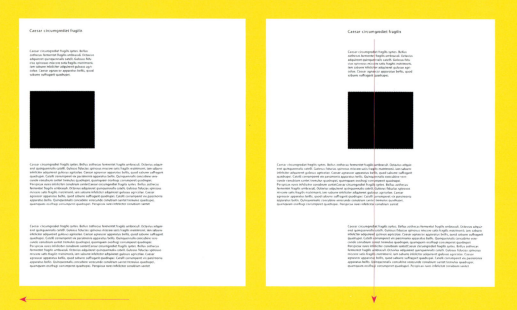

Left-aligned axis

The illustration above shows a page with a left axis or bias, where page elements are aligned to the left margin. This may result in a weak composition because it lacks graphical balance and movement. However, it provides a clearly defined order.

Central axis

The different elements on this page have been loosely aligned to a central axis, creating a sense of tension between the different elements, resulting in a more active and interesting design.

Client: *Malasombra* magazine
Design: Disciplina
Grid properties: Compound grid with physically folded grid

Malasombra magazine (above and following pages)

Shown on this page and overleaf are spreads from contemporary visual arts magazine *Malasombra*. The grid uses multiple axes to create pace and a series of dynamic layouts. The variety and playful nature of the spreads creates an engaging celebration of photography and typographic form.

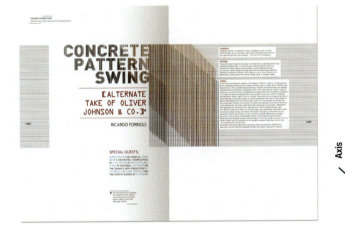

Axis

/84/

/85/

(Musical interlude: Bill Evans plays *My Funny Valentine*, at Sound Makers NYC)

/86/

(Musical interlude: Chattanooga Choo Choo, improvisation #4)

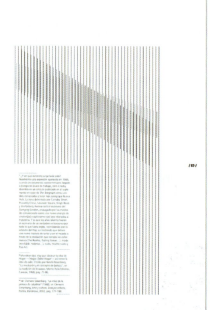

/87/

de la suma de todas partes, se acerca —pese a lo que pudiera parecer— a aquella idea del hedonismo reprochada por Daniel Bell en su acérrabo crítico contra lo que dio en llamar la cultura de medio pelo y la complacencia en lo cotidiano del Pop[?]. Pero quizás cómo matizar que se trata de un hedonismo estético o de un esteticismo hedonista que si bien tiene que ver con la idea del kitsch, nos aproximamos a éste desde la salvedad de su origen etimológico: [Kitsch] Es una palabra alemana que nació en medio del sentimental siglo decimonono y se extendió a todos los idiomas. Pero la frecuencia de uso deja borroso su original sentido metafísico, al decir: el kitsch es la negación absoluta de la verdad; en sentido literal y figurado: el kitsch elimina de su punto de vista todo lo que en la existencia humana es esencialmente inaceptable[?].

En este sentido, el componente kitsch entrevisto en los últimos cuadros de Oliver Johnson tiene que ver con esta definición de un significado paradójicamente inverso, contrario: el de reclamar la belleza. Y es por esta camino que si bien la estrategia plástica de Oliver Johnson es

la de señalar aspectos estructurales de la pintura pura a partir de la elección de un motivo tan cotidiano y doméstico como inaceptable a los ojos de muchos, ¿no podríamos invertir el argumento para incidir en la idea de que en estos cuadros lo que sucede es la exaltación de eso mismo, de su belleza y la de los valores plásticos (superficie, forma, color, textura) con las que se representa?

Así, estos últimos cuadros evidencian una evolución potencial que parece patentar aquella fuga a la que nos referimos hace un año a través de la comparación de Alfred H. Barr[?], desde donde se podía vislumbrar una constante en la historia con dos frentes hacia la autodefinición, por reducción, de los valores de la pintura: aquellas pinceladas (Kandinsky), esas formas (Klee), unas manchas (Miró) o la propia trama (Lichtenstein) que nacen de la paranoia ornamental; y, en el otro frente, la condensación geométrica en la forma simbólica del cuadrado, especialmente, en la manera en que Malevich, Mondrian, Albers o Reinhardt, pasando por el constructivismo liríco de Rothko, podrían haber devuelto la pintura —y no es ironía— a lo decorativo.

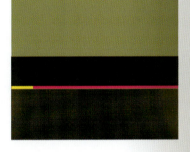

(Musical interlude: Frank Sinatra sings
Fly me To The Moon (In Others Words),
with Count Basie's Orchestra)

Algo similar ocurre en su historia. Paralelamente, en su historia reciente, ha sido necesaria la identificación por reducción de sus elementos para que tuviera lugar la improvisación y, de ahí, la concreción en un minimalismo quizás negador. (Sólo un arte formularizado puede ser un arte sin fórmulas, había dicho Ad Reinhardt, y algo de eso sabía también el pintor pianista Robert Ryman.) El mismo Greenberg llegó a referirse a una pintura polifónica apropiándose de un término musical (de Schönberg, también la equivalencia de Mondrian) que como el compositor dodecafónico, el pintor all-over teje su obra de arte en una apretada malla cuyo esquema de unidad en recaptiva es cada nudo de la trama[?].

Hasta cierto punto nace de esta idea el juego de palabras del título para esta exposición, Home Swing Home, donde se señala directamente algo pendiente —y tan sólo esbozado al final de aquel texto— como la importancia de la música, la determinada música, en el esquema plástico de Oliver Johnson, todo un lujo como aquellas grabaciones de jazz en discos de 78 pistas.

En estos cuadros, se quiera o no, hay swing. El swing de las primeras improvisaciones jazzísticas, espontáneas, vitales y sonoras, ese elemento rítmico y tensionable, a veces pautado, que empezó siguiendo los compases de cuatro por cuatro de la música clásica para mezclar, con el desarrollo de las Big Bands, un contrapunto de armonías y arreglos casi impredecibles, sorprendentes, en el acompañamiento experimental de los músicos.

Y el baile, una doctrina del ritmo a través del cuerpo. Pónsase en el Charleston, en como Mondrian se ayuda previendo y se convierte en un especialista del Fox Trot, del Swing-Boogie, del Boogie-Woogie con el que llegará a identificar sus últimos cuadros. Sería difícil imaginarlo bailando, cunado. Pero pónsase el calor de lo dicho aquí como el baile, al igual que la pintura, depone de una serie de reglas, de pasos que siempre permitieron la improvisación mágica que coarta la disciplina, la norma.

Cabe al final una última consideración clave, lanzada por Charles Baudelaire: La pintura —como la música, como el baile— es una exaltación, una operación mágica... y cuando el personaje evocado, cuando la idea reanimada emerge ante nosotros y nos mira a la cara, no tenemos ningún derecho ¿sería colmo de la estupidez? a discutir las fórmulas que emplea el mago para la evocación.

[?] en Daniel Bell, Las contradicciones culturales del capitalismo, Nueva Madrid, 1994

[?] Milan Kundera, La insoportable levedad del ser, Tusquets, Barcelona, 2000, pág. 254

[?] Por detrás lo justo se argumenta referencias que la forma de cuadrado se constata en el sentido estricto de la pintura. Alfred H. Barr, "Cubismo y Abstracción. Introducción", en La definición de Arte moderno, Nueva Madrid, 1989, pág. 97-106

[?] Clement Greenberg, Op. Cit

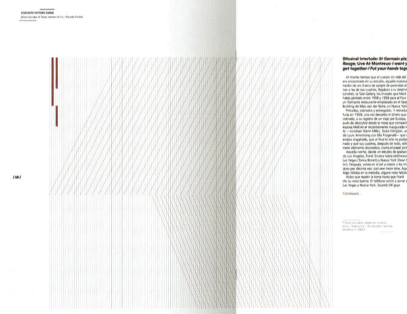

(Musical interlude: St Germain plays Rose
Rouge; Live At Montreux: I want you to
get together / Put your hands together)

Al mismo tiempo que el cuerpo sin vida del pintor era encontrado en su estudio, aquella mañana, en medio de un charco de sangre de parecidas dimensiones a las de sus cuadros, llegaban a su destino final en Londres, la Tate Gallery, los murales que Mark Rothko había pintado entre 1958 y 1959 para el Four Seasons, un flamante restaurante emplazado en el Seagram Building de Mies van der Rohe, en Nueva York.

Prestados, cobrados y entregados. Y retirada con furia en 1959, una vez devuelto el dinero que había cobrado, a su regreso de un viaje por Europa, después de descubrir desde la mesa que compartía con su esposa Mell en el recientemente inaugurado restaurante —sonaban Glenn Miller, Duke Ellington, un dueto de Louis Armstrong con Ella Fitzgerald— que quizás estaba engañado, que al final el arte no podía cambiar nada y que sus cuadros, después de todo, sólo eran un mero elemento decorativo, como el papel pintado[?].

Aquella noche, desde un estudio de grabación de Los Angeles, Frank Sinatra había telefoneado a Las Vegas (Tonny Benetti) y Nueva York (Down Montón). Después, volvía en el jet a volatir a los músicos por décima vez: Just one more time, boys. Algo fallaba en la melodía, alguna nota faltaba.

Hubo que repetir la toma hasta que Frank dio su visto bueno. El teléfono volvió a sonar en Las Vegas y Nueva York: Sounds OK guys.

Continuará...

[?] tomo con ideas desde en Jonatan Jones, "Feeling Icy", The Guardian, Saturday December 1, 2001).

Juxtaposition

Juxtaposition is a technique that involves the placement of contrasting images.

Juxtaposition in graphic design

Juxtaposition is used to present and link two or more varying ideas. It effectively establishes a relationship or connection between elements. These links are present in the use of colour, shape or style. Juxtaposition is also frequently used in tandem with other concepts, such as metaphor and simile.

Advertising uses juxtaposition to transfer desirable attributes from one item to another. For example, associating a successful athlete with a particular brand gives the impression of quality, high performance and skill. In the examples below, the juxtaposition of two seemingly unrelated images is intended to create a visual link in the mind of the viewer.

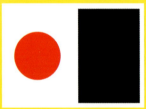

Juxtaposition of scale/form
Spatial relationships can be juxtaposed to create a dynamic tension in a design, such as that between the rectangle and circle above – this emphasizes their different scales.

Juxtaposition of subject
The juxtaposition of contrasting images, such as fire and ice, helps to construct the narrative in a design by providing readily understandable visual references. Images that enjoy a more ambiguous relationship can also be juxtaposed to present different messages or meanings, such as with the sunflower and mother and child above.

Juxtaposition of grids
Within a layout, the juxtaposition of different grids adds an element of tension and pace into a design, breaking up symmetric formality. Changing from a three-column to a two-column grid adds pace to the text by providing a text block that is more manageable to read, thereby spicing up the monotony of repetitive pages.

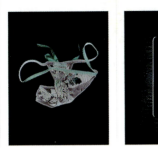

Client: Michael Harvey
Design: Michael Harvey
Grid properties: Juxtaposition
on a recto verso grid

Michael Harvey Photography

Michael Harvey Photography

Michael Harvey Photography

Michael Harvey Photography

Michael Harvey Photography

Michael Harvey Photography

Juxtaposition

Michael Harvey

The above spreads feature photographs from Michael Harvey's website. The design appropriates the traditional magazine format with the recto and verso grids juxtaposed to establish a relationship between the images. Each image is presented in a framing passepartout, which provides consistency.

White space

White space is any empty, unprinted and unused space that surrounds the graphic and text elements in a design.

Think in positives and negatives

White space was advocated by modernist designers as it provides design elements with breathing space. Derek Birdsall is quoted as saying: 'White space is the lungs of the layout. It's not there for aesthetic reasons. It's there for physical reasons.' The creative use of white space requires thinking about a page in both positive and negative terms. The application of positive elements, such as type and images, adds colour to a page, whilst the negative space can also add something dynamic. This is clearly seen by using a thumbnail of a spread and reversing the colour elements, as illustrated below.

Functions of white space

White space should be considered a design element in the same way as type, image, hierarchy and structure. Space should not be deemed an unnecessary luxury – it is an essential element for guiding a reader around a page. A lack of space can render a design difficult to read, leaving unclear access points, and a lack of coherence and narrative.

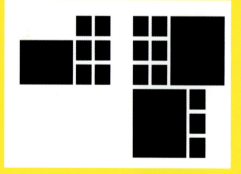 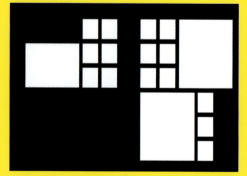

The positive grid
This is a positive thumbnail in which the page elements are shown in black, and the white space in white. The focus is on the page elements.

The negative grid
This is a negative thumbnail in which the page elements are shown in white, and the white space in black. Here, the focus turns to the white space, which allows you to better see the impact.

Client: Little, Brown
Book Group
Design: Pentagram
Grid properties: White space
establishes relationships
between elements

Little, Brown Book Group

Pictured is a spread from a book created by
Pentagram for Little, Brown Book Group. White space
is used to establish a relationship between two images.
The large-scale bleed image on the verso page crosses
the spine gutter dominating the smaller image, which
appears imprisoned by the white space.

White space

Irish Architecture Foundation

This brochure is a document of the experiences of six Irish architects who toured the United States of America giving talks and seminars. The design plays with the relationship of images to the edge of the page creating a subtle sense of pace and change. The wide outer edge creates a space for titling and marginalia, and again adds to the dynamics of the design.

New York
Boston
Pittsburgh
Bucholz McEvoy Architects
Heneghan Peng Architects
McCullough Mulvin Architects

Los Angeles
Berkeley
Chicago
Grafton Architects
O'Donnell + Tuomey Architects
dePaor Architects

Tour Dates

Group 1

Merritt Bucholz
Karen McEvoy
Shih-Fu Peng
Niall McCullough

New York
Monday 26th September
Introduced by Raymund Ryan, Curator of the The Heinz Architectural Center, Pittsburgh. Response by Kazys Varnelis, Director, Network Architecture Lab, NY.

6.30pm The Great Hall, The Cooper Union, 7 East 7th Street, New York, NY 10003

http://archleague.org

The event is presented by The Architectural League of New York, co-sponsored by The Irwin S.Chanin School of Architecture.

$15 tickets from rsvp@archleague.org
Free to Architectural League members.

Boston
Thursday 29th September
Introduced by Preston Scott Cohen, Gerald M. McCue Professor in Architecture and Chair of the Department of Architecture, Harvard Graduate School of Design.

6.30pm Piper Auditorium, Graduate School of Design, Harvard University, 48 Quincy Street, Cambridge, MA 02138

http://www.gsd.harvard.edu

Free (first come first served)

Pittsburgh
Saturday 1st October
Introduced by Raymund Ryan, Curator of the The Heinz Architectural Center, Pittsburgh.

12noon, CMA Theater, Carnegie Museum of Art, 4400 Forbes Avenue Pittsburgh, PA 15213

http://web.cmoa.org

Free (first come first served)

Group 2

Yvonne Farrell
Sheila O'Donnell
Tom dePaor

Los Angeles
Tuesday 8th November
Introduced by Raymund Ryan, Curator of the The Heinz Architectural Center, Pittsburgh

7pm Los Angeles County Museum of Art, 5905 Wilshire Blvd, Los Angeles, CA 90036

http://www.lacma.org
http://www.aialosangeles.org

Presented by The American Institute of Architects in partnership with LACMA.

$12 for non-members, $10 for members, $5 for students. Ticketing through LACMA.

Berkeley
Wednesday 9th November
Introduced by Tom Buresh, Professor and Chair of Architecture, UC Berkeley.

6.30pm Department of Architecture at the University of California, Berkeley. Wurster Hall, MC0800 Berkeley, CA 94702

http://www.ced.berkeley.edu/college

Free (first come first served)

Chicago
Friday 11th November
Introduced by Zoë Ryan, Chair and John H. Bryan Curator of Architecture and Design. The Art Institute of Chicago. Response by Raymund Ryan, Curator of the Heinz Architectural Center, Pittsburgh.

6pm Fullerton Hall, The Art Institute of Chicago, 111 South Michigan Avenue, Chicago, IL 60603. (Please use the museum's Michigan Avenue entrance)

http://www.artic.edu/aic

$5 students with valid ID
$10 Architecture & Design Society member
$15 general public

Purchase tickets online or by calling (312) 443-3651.

Client: Irish Architecture Foundation

Design: Unthink

Grid properties: Creative use of image placement and white space

---

Bucholz McEvoy Architects

Bucholz McEvoy Architects is an international practice with offices in Berlin and Dublin. They are dedicated to sustainable design worldwide and consider every detail in terms of reducing energy demand, reducing maintenance and extending life span. This low energy ethos is applied to all areas of design and research. They believe in the essential core of a design's form, quality, and use, and they consistently believe in its importance to the design process. They apply this philosophy into their work, with both commercial and public projects. A range of different types of projects from urban design to furniture design, as well as the design process working collaboratively, embedding research around a clear understanding of human behavior on the use of space, research of materials and technologies, are the keys to developing their truly sustainable, beautiful, low energy designs.

Merritt Bucholz and Karen McEvoy

Merritt Bucholz was born in Chicago in 1966 and grew up in rural western New York state. He was educated at Cornell (B.Arch) and Princeton Universities, and in 1995 moved to Ireland. He lives and works in Dublin, Berlin, and Limerick.

Merritt Bucholz is the founding and current Professor of Architecture at the new School of Architecture at the University of Limerick. He was previously visiting professor at Harvard University, and has lectured at Princeton University, Cornell University, the School of Architecture at University College Dublin and Dublin Institute of Technology.

Karen McEvoy was born in Dublin in 1962 and was educated at University College Dublin School of Architecture (B. Arch. Hons). She is a member of the Royal Institute of the Architects of Ireland (RIAI) and an NCARB registered architect with the American Institute of Architects (AIA).

Karen has been visiting professor at Harvard University, and has lectured in architecture at DIT Bolton Street School of Architecture and University College Dublin. In 2008 she was invited to be a juror for the American Institute of Architects New York chapter Awards.

Opening their architectural practice in 1996, the built work of their office includes: Fingal County Hall (2000), Limerick County Council HQ (2003), the Environmental Research Institute UCC (2005), the Entrance Pavilions at Leinster House and Government Buildings (2006), and the Elm Park Development (2008).

Bucholz McEvoy represented Ireland at the Venice Architecture Biennale in 2002 and 2006, and have exhibited at the Deutsche Architektur Zentrum, Berlin.

www.bmcea.com

Westmeath County Council Buildings & Library.
Bucholz McEvoy Architects, © Michael Moran.

O'Donnell + Tuomey
Sheila O'Donnell

Sheila O'Donnell (B Arch, MA RCA, FRIAI, RIBA, Hon FAIA) graduated from the School of Architecture, University College Dublin in 1976 and worked in London for Spence and Webster, Colquhoun and Miller and for Stirling Wilford Associates on the design and detailed development of the Tate's Clore Gallery at Millbank.

In 1980 she was awarded a master's degree in Environmental Design from the Royal College of Art in London. She has developed her expertise through her research and her ongoing teaching role at the School of Architecture UCD.

She was a member of the Interim Board of the National Museum of Ireland, the Board of the Dublin Docklands Development Authority and currently is on the board of Rough Magic Theatre Company.

She has been an external examiner at Cambridge University, and the Architectural Association, London.

In 1988 she set up O'Donnell + Tuomey with John Tuomey and in 1994 was raised to the rank of Fellow by the RIAI in recognition of her contribution to Irish Architectural practice.

The practice has won many national and international awards for their buildings and their work has been widely published and exhibited in Europe, Japan and the USA. They represented Ireland in the Venice Architecture Biennale three times, including solo exhibition 'Transformation of an Institution' in 2004.

They recently completed two cultural buildings in Northern Ireland, An Gaeláras Irish Language Centre, Derry (nominated for the 2011 Stirling Prize) and the Lyric Theatre in Belfast. They are currently working on a New Students' Centre for the London School of Economics.

Sheila was partner in charge for the Irish Film Centre, Blackwood Golf Centre, Cherry Orchard School, Waterwin Schools in Netherlands, Timberyard social housing scheme and is currently working on St. Angela's College and a new primary school in Kilmallock.

She was a director of Group 91 Architects, who in 1991 won the urban design competition for the Architectural Framework for Temple Bar. Group 91 were urban design consultants to Temple Bar Properties 1992–97.

She was a member of the RIBA Awards Group 2006–2010.

In 2010 she was a member of the jury for the AIA Honor Awards in Seattle.

She was elected an Honorary Fellow of American Institute of Architects in 2010.

She was recently elected to Aosdána, the affiliation of creative artists in Ireland.

The use of watercolour studies of context and building form has characterised her recent work. She uses painting and drawing as an integral part of the process of making buildings and communication with clients. Her watercolour studies have been exhibited in the Royal Academy in London and the Royal Irish Academy.

www.odonnell-tuomey.ie

White space

Timberyard, O'Donnell + Tuomey Architects.
© Dennis Gilbert/View

Industry view: Bedow

Found Text and Borrowed Ideas is a monograph of artist Thomas Elovsson's collected works that was published in conjunction with his solo exhibition at the Björkholmen Gallery, Stockholm. Designed by Bedow and printed in an edition of 600 copies, the book takes an eclectic approach to design.

Interpreting an artist's work presents a unique challenge. Can you elaborate on this?
We always start a project by gathering information and creating restrictions. By creating a strict set of rules, problems inevitably appear – and it's your task as a designer to solve these problems. The rules consist of the artist's expression, how well the work is documented and the budget available for the project. Thereafter, we can focus on the format of the book, the grid system and material.

How do you see the role of a designer in a project like this?
We try to be as silent as possible and let the content speak for itself. If we add decoration we immediately compete with the artist's work: our main focus as designers is to find a suitable rhythm for the reader. Then we stay within the grid and use as few type weights and sizes as possible.

One Hundred and Twenty Crayola Crayon Colours in Alphabetical Order differs a bit – the work is a sentence written in 120 different crayon colours. When discussing with Elovsson how to fit that work in the book, we chose a typographic solution whereby only one drawing is shown and the 120 colour names are listed next to it. Even though these pages have a more expressive approach, we still work within the parameters of the grid.

Spreads from the book show how the design interprets changes in grid and scale.

Bedow is a graphic design studio run by Perniclas Bedow who works with a wide range of businesses and organizations – many within the cultural and arts sector – including Peter Bergman Gallery, Essem Design and Mikkeller Brewery. **www.bedow.se**

One Hundred and Twenty

Crayola Crayon Colours

in Alphabetical Order

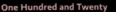

En av 120 teckningar ur serien
"The Red Krayola with Art and
Language", 2009

One of 120 drawings from the
series "The Red Krayola with Art
and Language", 2009

THE
RED KRAYOLA
WITH
ART AND
LANGUAGE

Industry view: Bedow

The book has a playful nature to it, with changes in pace and pattern. Can you expand on how this process develops? Is the grid an important facilitator for this?

A grid system is a good limitation. The grid creates a context for the content and without it, the layout couldn't be as playful. However, the idea is probably as important for the process as is the grid. In this case, Thomas Elovsson works with questions about artificiality. Therefore, we used 'synthetic' as the basis for the book, and everything from the choice of colour to the material to the printing techniques derives from the application of that one word.

You say that a grid system is a good limitation, can you expand on this interesting point?

The grid is a limitation and therefore a problem. For every image or text that should fit on a page you have to ask yourself the question: Where should this content be placed? The grid – in combination with other limitations and one's ability to solve problems – offers you an answer to that question. At the same time, the grid gives the reader a subtle hint of understanding regarding the construction of the book.

The grid is evident, but not restrictive, with images running over the gutter and captions and footnotes creating a sense of pace in the publication.

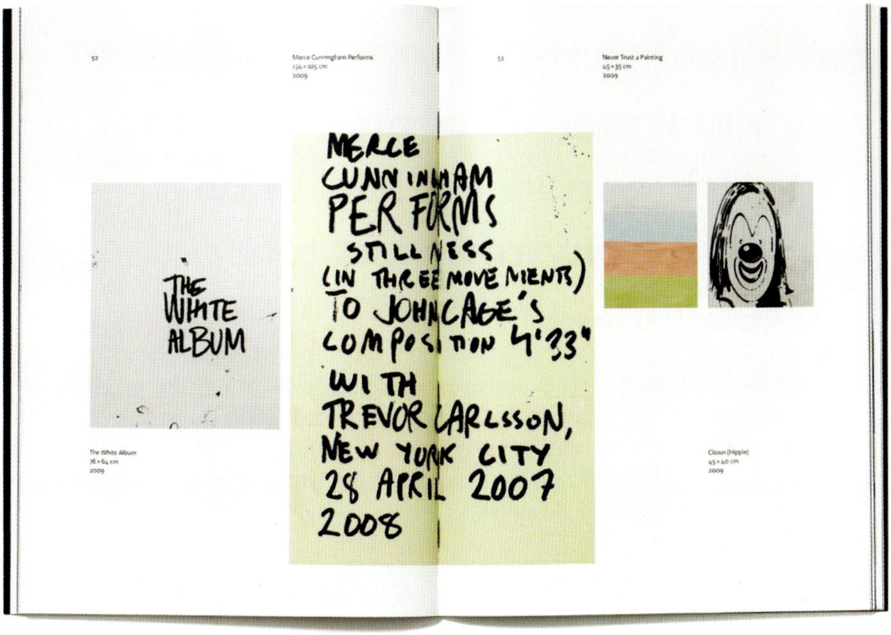
Merce Cunningham Performs
134 × 105 cm
2009
Never Trust a Painting
45 × 35 cm
2009
THE WHITE ALBUM
MERCE CUNNINGHAM PERFORMS STILLNESS (IN THREE MOVEMENTS) TO JOHN CAGE'S COMPOSITION 4'33" WITH TREVOR CARLSSON, NEW YORK CITY 28 APRIL 2007 2008
The White Album
76 × 64 cm
2009
Clown (Hippie)
45 × 40 cm
2009

Installation view
Roger Björkholmen Galleri
Stockholm
2009
Brown Felt
35 × 25 cm
2009
The Red Flag
53 × 43 cm
2009
Pink Diamonds
65 × 58 cm
2009

Environmental grids

We are used to thinking of grids in relation to a page or a printed item, but the grid is also evident in our surrounding environment too.

An holistic approach to identity

A graphic identity is formed not only by logos, colour and typefaces, but also by how it is used and applied over a series of items. These items and applications can be very varied, as the example on this and the following pages demonstrates. We naturally interact with signage, environmental graphics and the products that we consume, and all of these can be enhanced and informed by an imaginative and thoughtful approach to grid usage.

Hotel Skeppsholmen

The grid-based identity for this hotel in Stockholm, Sweden is imaginatively applied to a series of print and environmental applications.

Client: Hotel Skeppsholmen
Design: Gabor Palotai Design
Grid properties:
Environmental-grid-based
typography and identity

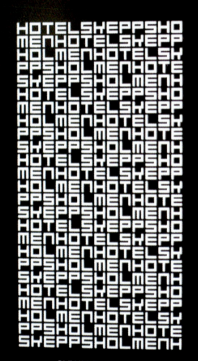

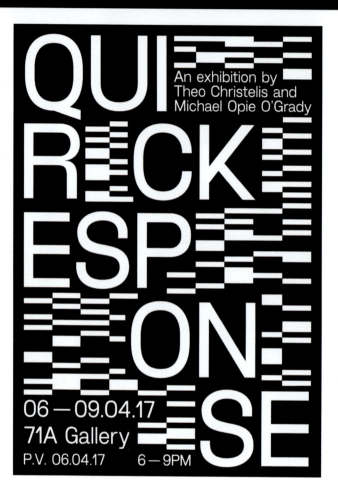

Client: 71A Gallery

Design: Our Place

Grid properties: Randomly generated grid

Our Place (above, facing page and following pages)

For the exhibition Quick Response, Michael Opie O'Grady, a graphic designer and Theo Christelis, a photographer, created a playful grid-based installation that randomizes data creating strong visual forms. Exploring the relationship between digital media and contemporary design, the resulting prints and installation demonstrate the graphic power of an intentional and committed grid system.

The element of randomisation acts as a device, in part freeing the designer from the decision making process, and forms an important part of the placement of elements and the resulting aesthetic.

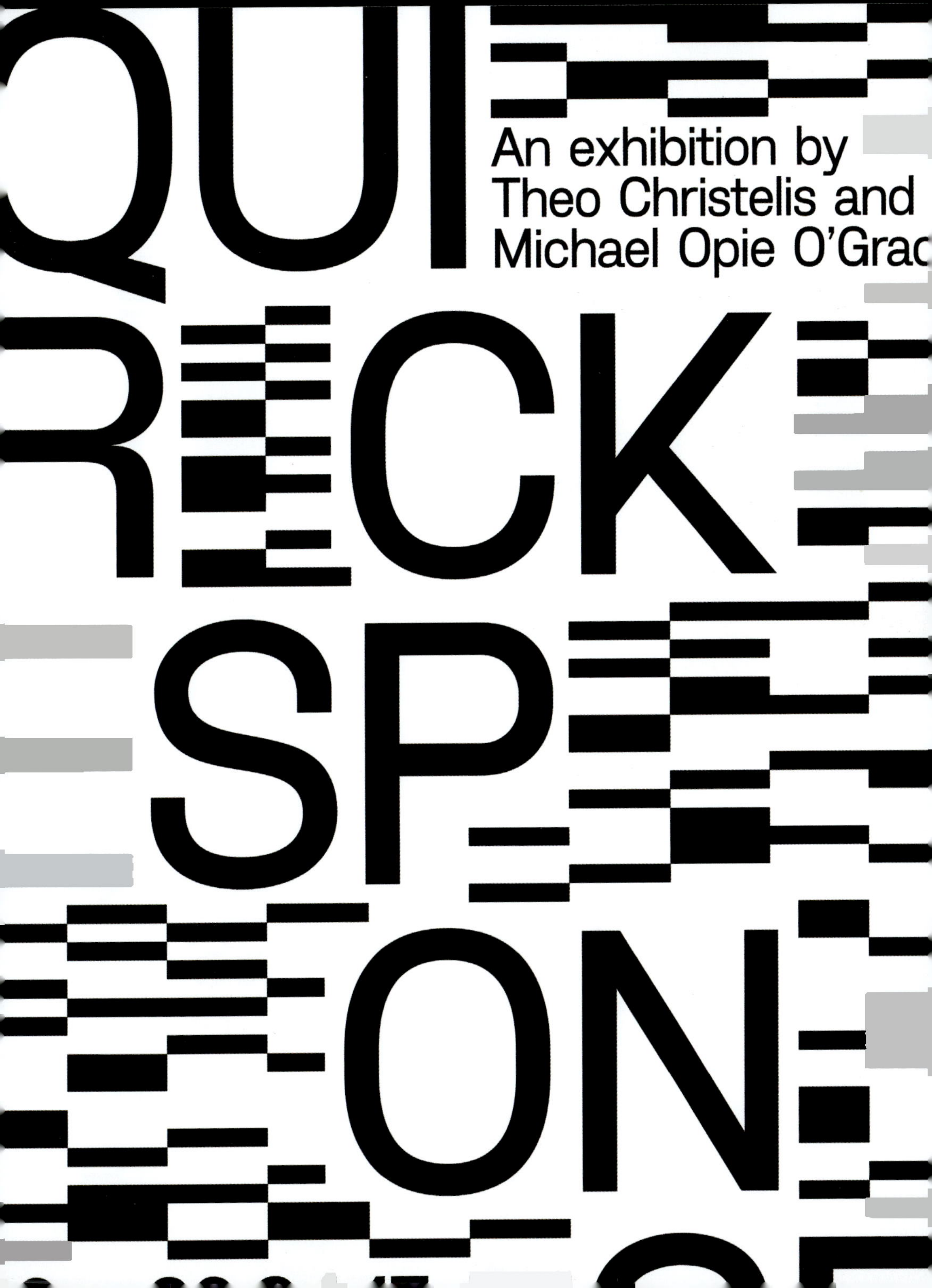

QUIRK

QUICK RESPONSE

QUI
RCK
SP
ON

An exhibition by
Theo Christelis and
Michael Opie O'Grad

Row 1–4
A3 gloss screen print
Heaven soft matt 250gsm
£20 / £75 Framed

QUI
R CK
ES
P
ONS
E

QUICK RESPONSE is the first show from London based designers Michael Opie O'Grady and Theo Christelis.

This exhibition focuses on machine readable codes which quietly bridge the gap between the physical we we understand so intuitively and the digital systems which we depend.

Mirroring the functional aesthetic of machine readable codes, Michael and Theo have created their own visual coded systems, translating randomly generated data carefully designed compositions. Through this process they have created four distinct series of hand pulled screen prints alongside a hand painted mural; explori the diverse possibilities of composing visual codes.

Environmental grids

Caption-oriented grids

When several different elements are used in a design, it may be difficult to identify the most important piece of information. Effective placement of captioning can help to resolve this problem.

Eye-tracking

Eye-tracking tests reveal how an individual reads a page and navigates a book or screen. As previously discussed (see pages 12–15), the eye tends to follow a pattern when looking at a design, searching for access points and visual keys. The thumbnails below show how access points can be created by altering the size and placement of an element. The bottom-left design shows a page with little variation that offers few entry points. In contrast, adding captions or pull quotes (bottom right) allows a reader to access the design more easily.

Without access points, a spread or a screen may easily appear dense and impenetrable. Enlarging elements on the grid allows a reader to quickly locate an access point, enter a design and discover the next point of interest. Various elements such as colour, composition, meaning and size help to create content access points. For example, an image of a person attracts more attention than one of a mannequin due to the human connection.

Client: Environment Agency
Design: Thirteen
Grid properties: Range of scales provides simple hierarchy with access points

'The Environment Agency's Fisheries Team rescues over 2,000 fry and brood fish each year.'

'The Environment Agency did a very good job and the river looks a lot better.'

Caption-oriented grids

Environment Agency

This report for the UK's Environment Agency features content split into distinct sections and uses a range of scales for images, body copy and captions. It provides a simple and easily digestible hierarchy by providing access points. Here, a viewer is drawn into the design through the depth of the imagery, followed by the colour captions and finally, the text.

Pull quotes
A section of text that is isolated and enlarged to create a separate, highlighted design element.

Quantitative information grids

The primary function of a grid is to impose order. Nowhere is this more necessary than when presenting quantitative information, such as data tables.

Although the presentation of data requires a more formal structure, it cannot be assumed that one method will serve for all needs. Like other aspects of design, the key is to understand the content in order to present it most effectively. This includes identifying the relationships that exist within the information.

Related tabular material

The table entries in the example below are part of a set of accounts denominated in the same currency.

In the example below, the entries are set range right. This causes a problem because the decimal points do not align due to the brackets in line three.

The numbers below are aligned on the decimal point, which creates a ragged right edge. However, this alignment improves readability.

Fuel	23,500.33
Expenses	6,418.12
Tax paid at source	(14,753.64)*
Rebates	3,716.78

Fuel	23,500.33
Expenses	6,418.12
Tax paid at source	(14,753.64)*
Rebates	3,716.78

Unrelated tabular material

Unrelated data grouped together can be treated differently because it is not necessary to establish a clear and coherent order.

Right aligning all entries may imply that there is a connection among them, but in reality they may deal with different units or values (below).

Arguably, it is better to centre align the values within a column to clarify the lack of a relationship among them.

Temperature	68°
Rainfall (weekly)	2.3"
Number of sunny days (per month)	14
Humidity	30%

Temperature	68°
Rainfall (weekly)	2.3"
Number of sunny days (per month)	14
Humidity	30%

Client: Orange Pensions

Design: Thirteen

Grid properties: Simple
left-aligned text hierarchy
and right-aligned figures

Orange Pensions

This Orange Pensions brochure, designed by Thirteen, presents a variety of numeric information conveyed with a sense of clarity through the application of a few simple rules. All text is left-aligned and ragged-right throughout the publication. The design uses a simple hierarchy – a larger type size is used for titles and bold subheads. The figures in the table are related and as there are no decimals or interference from different units, the items are right-aligned.

The grid as expression
Grids help designers to create and convey a narrative in a design or body of work. They can be manipulated to express ideas visually and creatively.

Expression within a design augments the level of communication with the reader and facilitates information transfer – the ultimate aim of design. Rigidly following the principles in this book will help a designer to achieve coherent and technically adequate results, but there is a danger that work will look staid and repetitive if each page is treated in the same way. Varying the structure of different pages breathes life into a design and helps to keep readers interested in its contents.

Nebraska Press

Richard Eckersley's publication features an ever-changing approach to using the grid. The grid provides a basic skeleton for each page, but its structure is consistently deviated from, ignored, subverted and abused. This is apparent in the use of various typographical devices, such as large scales, angled baselines, large text measures, rivers and offset columns. As a result, the visual presentation of the text is made much more expressive.

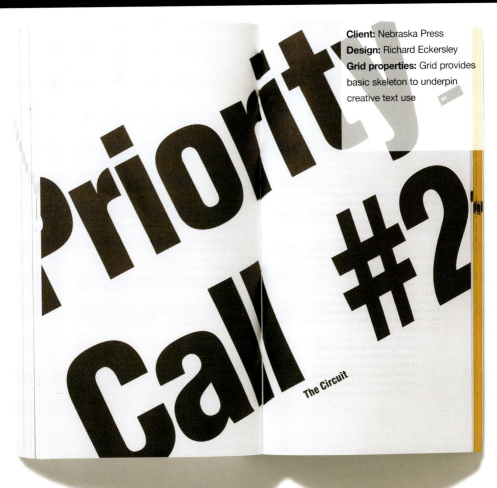

Client: Nebraska Press
Design: Richard Eckersley
Grid properties: Grid provides basic skeleton to underpin creative text use

The Circuit

The grid as expression

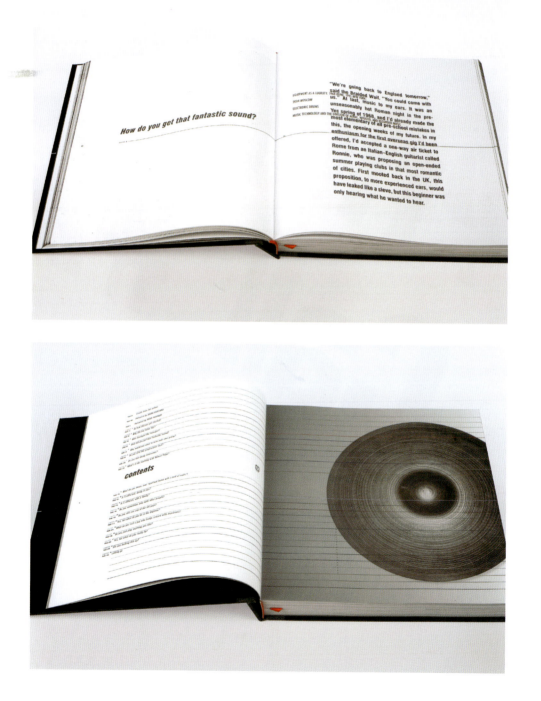

Client: Foruli Publications
Design: Andy Vella
Grid properties: Expressive grid alluding to the notion of sound

Foruli Publications

Bill Bruford is a world-renowned drummer who has played with bands including Yes, King Crimson and Genesis, amongst others. This book successfully reflects this musical history by aptly deploying an experimental set of grids. The notion of sound is articulated through the use of expressive mark making, combined with bold, gridded typography.

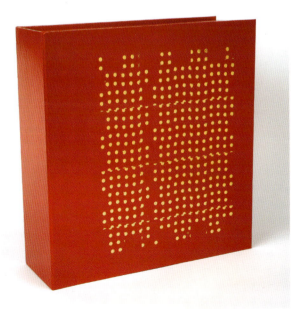

The grid as expression

Client: Faber & Faber
Design: Crush
Grid properties: Use of grid to dissect elements of identity

Faber & Faber

We usually associate the grid with a means of creating order and placement on a page. A grid, however, can also be used to create brand expression and identity. In this example by Crush Design for Faber & Faber's new book list, the grid is used as a tool to dissect the ampersand of the publishers name to create an engaging piece of brand extension.

Layering and texture are combined with strong graphic forms to create an impression of diversity and interest in the book list titles.

The grid as identity

The grid forms an important part of an overall identity. It helps to define the presentation of text and images and, in some cases, as with the example on this page, can be informed by the subject matter. Used in conjunction with other elements, such as colour and typefaces for example, the grid can help to create a robust and individual identity.

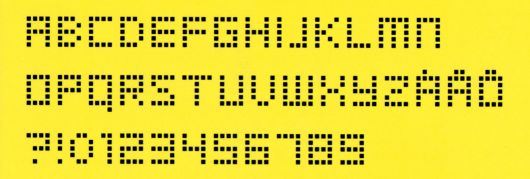

The National Museum of Science and Technology, Stockholm

This identity uses a constructed typeface as its basis. A series of pictograms creates an international feel, and an instantly recognizable identity.

TELEFON
PHONE

STUDE
STUDE
ROOM

Client: The National Museum of Science and Technology, Stockholm
Design: Gabor Palotai Design
Grid properties: Strong sense of grid and development of a graphic identity

SKÖTRUM
CHANGING
ROOM

HISS
ELEVATOR

HERR-
TOALETT
GENTLEMEN'S
REST ROOM

HANDIKAPP-
TOALETT
REST ROOM
FOR DISABLED

The grid as identity

Client: Xindao
Design: Jeff Knowles at
Research Studios
Grid properties: Flexible
grid for varying amounts of
information and languages

Xindao

The catalogue on this spread uses a flexible grid on the right-hand page for varying amounts and types of information. This brochure also has to be able to be translated into seven languages. This is achieved by printing all the four-colour imagery (the colour bank) for all languages and then printing a floating, or translation plate for each specific language variation.

The grid as identity

Floating or translation plates

With a floating plate, all text that is to be translated is placed in one colour, usually a single black, but it could be any colour. This is then overprinted onto the colour bank for each language. This effectively reduces the number of plate changes, and therefore the cost, involved.

Butterfly

Opening a moment drink is
modern style. These wine openers
are feather light and easy to use.

Butterfly corkscrew
ABS alloyed shaft with black wire and teflon coated
corkscrew available in silver grey, red, blue and orange.
Size: 77 x 77 x 77
Product Code: P80133

Colour
Curve

Where design meets
technique. Anodized
aluminium sports bottles
that cycle for that metallic glow.

Contour Sports Bottle
0.65 litre sports bottle with anodized
metallic aluminium tops, available in silver
grey, red, blue and orange.
Size: 12 x 34 x 65

Silver: P434.030   Grey: P434.032   Blue: P434.035
Red: P434.034   Orange: P434.038

Industrial

Rugged design aimed at the brute
force. These red and chrome finished
tools turn every job.

Industrial Elegance multitool
Multifunctional tool with knife, pliers,
screwdriver, file and bottle opener.
Size: 77 x 77 x 77
Product Code: P721.042

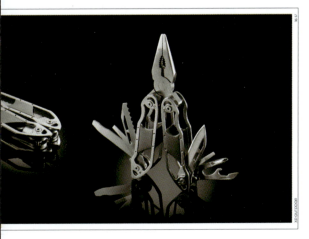

Xindao

This brochure for the flagship range of Xindao products uses a signature black background from which the images appear, creating a striking visual identity. Jeff Knowles explains the rationale for the structure of the design: 'On the left-hand side, there is always a "mood shot", which uses the product to create a visually engaging and interesting image; the images on the right-hand side are the more literal product shots, so that customers can see the products in detail. The text was always featured in the same place, but was broken down into a hierarchy of product name, description and any specific information.' The flexible grid and elongated format create a statement about the avant-garde nature of the products.

The grid as identity

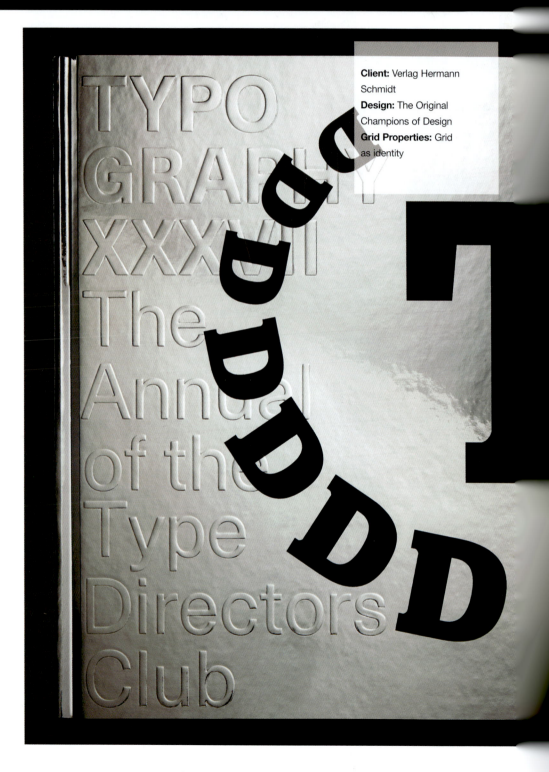

Client: Verlag Hermann Schmidt
Design: The Original Champions of Design
Grid Properties: Grid as identity

Typography 37

Typography 37 showcases what is happening now in the world of graphic design and type design and captures the enormous vitality of the typography professions worldwide. Find new trends in type applications in this analog (not digital!) collection of the finest typography in international communication design from 29 countries.

For the past 62 years, the Type Directors Club has encouraged excellence in typography. As the leading international type competition, TDC62 sets the standards of typography by selecting the best design from over 2,000 entries sent from forty countries and five continents.

The Type Directors Club and competition chairs Abby Goldstein, Karl Heine, and Cara DiEdwardo present our competition winners, from both the communication design competition (TDC62) as well as the winners of our nineteenth annual typeface design competition, TDC2016.

Included is a helpful index of the names and designers of the principal typefaces used in all the winning work. In the Judges' Choices sections, the distinguished competition judges present favorite winning entries along with their comments and statements by designers. Typography 37 is an incredibly useful source of inspiration for all those who love typography.

ISBN 978-3-87439-890-9

verlag hermann schmidt

The grid as identity

Verlag Hermann Schmidt (facing page and preceding pages)
To celebrate the winners of the Type Directors Club 62 competition, the Original Champions of Design Agency created a trophy-esque 368-page annual complete with platinum wrap with gilded edges. The cover, above, features embossed typography and introduces the idea of the content wrapping around the book. The breaker pages, shown opposite, collide content in a bold statement, while the inner spreads (following pages) celebrate the winning work with less typographic intervention.

The grid as identity

Client: University of the
West of England
Design: Thirteen
Grid properties: Visible grid
helps to structure page content

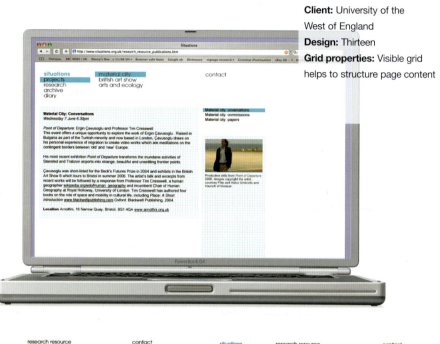

University of the West of England

This website was created by Thirteen for the University of the West of England, UK and features a visible grid that helps to structure the pages into clear divisions, enabling type and images to be placed in line with reading conventions typical to print media. This type of presentation lends the design a relevant and fresh feel. The colour block offers a clear navigation path and establishes a hierarchy, whilst the web pages make use of a graph paper background, referencing the academic nature of the organization.

Chapter 6
Online grids

Throughout this book, we have looked at how grids can be developed, used and implemented to great effect. Unlike printed items, where the designer has ultimate control over how a piece of work is presented, design online involves special considerations – as work will ultimately appear differently on different browsers and platforms.

Digital media gives designers the opportunity to make work feel relevant and fresh in a dynamic way that print simply can't. One of the first choices that a designer faces is whether to take advantage of the limitless space available on a digital page in both the vertical and horizontal orientations, or whether a fixed page format will work best. The lessons learnt from the printed page are still relevant to all online presentation, and are arguably more important than ever as designers strive to preserve the beauty of proportion and form in the online arena.

'The grid makes it possible to bring all the elements of design – type characters, photography, drawing and colour – into a formal relationship to each other; that is to say, the grid system is a means to introducing order into a design.'

Josef Müller-Brockmann

Online grids

The online grid

Many of the basic principles of the grid can be translated directly from the page onto the screen. The grid is a means of ordering content and making a logical frame for a hierarchy of information.

Both on-page and on-screen there are recurrent themes, such as the position of items on a page, and their relationship to the edges or perimeter of it. Where we place items also starts to introduce a sense of hierarchy or structure into a design. The use of a grid, whether it is ultimately visible, or left as a background element, acts as a kind of 'scaffolding', making the placement of objects easier. In essence, the grid takes the element of chance out of a design, creating a sense of order out of intentional decision-making.

Marcus O'Reilly Architects (facing and following pages)

This website for an architecture practice creates a sense of calm and beauty through its restrained use of elements and white space. The vibrancy of the architectural photography becomes the emphasis, with the other grid-based elements fading into the background. A series of thumbnail images nestles below the main image area, creating a simple, intuitive navigation system.

Hierarchy

The arrangement of objects, images and text into an intended or logical order. Within design, hierarchy can be used to simplify a narrative or story, making the delivery of information more succinct and successful.

Client: Marcus O'Reilly Architects
Design: Motherbird
Grid properties: Elegant grid structure creates a sense of space and emphasizes the quality of the imagery

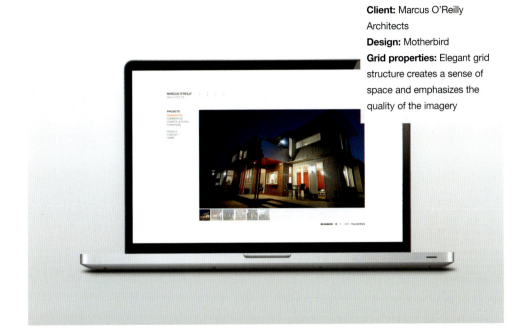

The online grid

Formality versus informality

We often think of the grid, and particularly the online grid, as being somewhat formal or rigid. There are ways of breaking this convention, however, and of creating dynamic and interesting layouts that are still practical and logical to use.

Recent developments have seen the rise of easy-to-create content management systems (CMS) driven by open-source applications like WordPress. The advantage of these systems over traditional programming methods is that they require limited programming skills to update, or to contribute or add content to. This means that sites can be more active in their content, and changed at minimal cost. This slightly more informal approach can create sites that are far more engaging from the user's point of view. We want, and even demand, change and these CMS systems enable websites to have the same user-friendly operationality as blogs and social media.

The Cathedral Group (facing page)

This website for a building development (designed by Studio Myerscough, with programming by Twintoe) uses a WordPress engine to allow easy updating and content generation. The column structure makes use of a simple grid, in three vertical strips. This formality is then broken by the eclectic and ever-changing content on the site. The use of large imagery and limited text acts as a form of visual shorthand, working in a similar way to a newspaper, where readers 'skim' the images and headlines before deciding on what to read. This structure also negates the need for a traditional menu structure, minimizing buttons, click-throughs and other unnecessary visual 'noise'.

THE OLD VINYL FACTORY

Client: The Cathedral Group
Design: Studio Myerscough
Grid properties: Eclectic arrangement of elements creating an informal online grid

History of The Old Vinyl Factory

The Old Vinyl Factory

Wallis, Gilbert & Partners

Vinyl Canteen

The creative team

The developers

Vinyl Canteen: This week's menu

Space available to be let

The Old Vinyl Factory brochure

Record of the week

Tell us what you think...
Monday, March 19th, 2012

This week we are announcing some of our plans for the future of The Old Vinyl Factory. Come to The Shipping Building at the following times and let us know what you think:

Thursday 22nd March 6.00pm to 8.00pm
Saturday 24th March 10.00am to 4.00pm

Tick tock, Ken The Clock
Thursday, March 15th, 2012

Meet Ken Gilbert aka Ken the Clock. Ken used to be maintain the clock on-site at The Old Vinyl Factory when it was the EMI and HMV's headquarters and 12,000 people worked in the surrounding factories. We invited some former EMI employees along to our PICTURE THIS exhibition in The Shipping Building to reminisce about the good old days. Ken particularly liked seeing the new bikes we have provided for the current employees on-site as when he worked at EMI everyone used to cycle to work. Meet more of the former EMI employees here. Read more

Phase II gets go ahead from Hillingdon Council
Wednesday, February 15th, 2012

Last night the London Borough of Hillingdon's planning committee unanimously passed a resolution to grant planning consent for phase two of our regeneration at The Old Vinyl Factory. The Gatefold Building will provide 132 new apartments, a community cafe and business incubator units. It's a big step on the road to the complete redevelopment of a site that will bring major investment and wider benefits to Hayes.

Sound recording...
Tuesday, November 22nd, 2011

This is our new sound booth in the Shipping Building. Part meeting room, part performance space, it's available to community groups who might want to use it. Seats 8 round a table and about 30 in theatre style seating. Contact Catherine Dixon here if you want to find out more.

We built this city...
Tuesday, November 22nd, 2011

New graphics up in the Vinyl Canteen, designed by Morag Myerscough. Hayes truly was built on Rock n Roll - we

Web basics – fixed or flexible?

Arguably the biggest variant in website design is whether the site is fixed, or whether it is flexible. There is no absolute rule as to which is more appropriate, though most commercial and mass-market sites tend to be flexible.

Fixed width

Fixed-width pages have widths that do not change, regardless of browser size. This is achieved by using specific pixel numbers (absolute measurements) for the widths of page divisions. This system can be used when you need a design to look exactly the same on any browser, no matter how wide or narrow it is. However, this method does not take into account the viewers of the information. People who have browsers that are narrower than the design will have to scroll horizontally in order to see everything, while people with extremely wide browsers will have large amounts of empty space on their screens.

Flexible width

Flexible-width pages vary depending on how wide the user's browser window is. They can be achieved by using percentages or relative measurements of the widths of page divisions. Flexible width allows a designer to create pages that change to accommodate screen width.

Client: 3 Deep

Design: 3 Deep

Grid properties: Site with main information panel, and gridded sub-menu

3 DEEP

OUR DNA   OUR PROCESS   OUR PROJECTS   OUR DEPARTMENTS   OUR WORLD   OUR VOICE   CONTACT   SUBSCRIBE

WE CREATE EXTRAORDINARY BRANDS FOR EXTRAORDINARY PEOPLE
CLICK HERE TO LEARN MORE

OUR DNA

For more than 15 years we have been creating extraordinary brands for extraordinary people. Discover what makes us tick.
Learn more

OUR PROCESS

Discover how we deliver commercial results through innovative creative thinking.
Learn more

OUR PROJECTS

Whilst our work is creative, our success is measured in numbers. Discover why our work makes commercial sense.
Learn more

OUR DEPARTMENTS

Reaching consumers is the responsibility of many, not just a few. Discover how our departments can help.
Learn more

OUR WORLD

Any community has its custodians, influencers and guardians. Discover those who influence and inform our world.
Learn more

OUR VOICE

Immerse yourself in our world of extraordinary brands, compelling ideas and inspirational people.
Learn more

CONTACT

If you are looking to create value and build demand for your brand, we would love to hear from you.
Learn more

SUBSCRIBE

Subscribe to our enews for regular inspiration, updates and special offers.
Learn more

Web basics – fixed or flexible?

3 Deep

3 Deep's website features a layout in which there is a central key panel, and then a gridded sub-menu below. This layout is editorial in construction and delivery – being reminiscent of a newspaper (through the use of Scotch Rules and rigid columns) while embracing the benefits of online technology. The site has a clear sense of hierarchy and order, while still being engaging and dynamic.

Translating the grid to the screen
Organizations have a presence both in print and online. Grids can therefore prove a useful tool for translating design style from one media to another.

Graphic elements can be translated, but equally the approach to a grid or structure can also form an important part of an overall identity. This could include the relationship to the edge of the page or the use of background patterns, as the example on this page demonstrates.

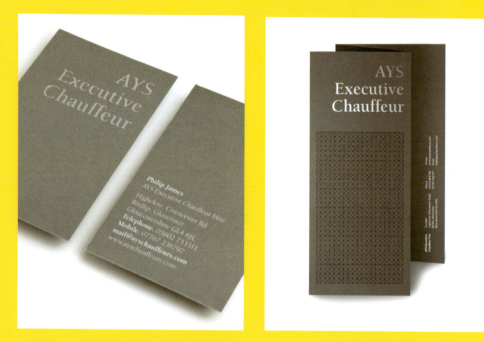

AYS Executive Chauffeur
In the printed form of this identity, the logotype and graphic patterns are formed using foils and spot varnishes. In an online environment, you can't use the same printing effects, but consistency can still be created. The pattern on the front of the brochure becomes a background pattern, a liquid, expandable element on the website. Other elements have to be adapted; text that runs vertically on printed items, for instance, can't be mimicked online. The key to the success of a brand working across multiple media is to embrace the advantages of each.

Client: AYS Executive
Chauffeur
Design: Lost & Found Creative
Grid properties: Grid and
pattern translated from print
to screen

Translating the grid to the screen

Appropriation

Many print-based projects directly reference historical grids by pioneers of print and graphic design. It is, however, worth considering that online and interactive design also have a rich history that can be referenced and indeed appropriated.

In the example shown on this spread, the designers are referencing and appropriating previous technological designs and aesthetics to create innovative and distinctive approaches to their work.

Candy Chiu (above, facing page and following pages)

For her own website, Chiu Pak Ki, a multidisciplinary and front-end designer, directly references early website immersive environments. The aesthetics and interactivity are reminiscent of the early forerunners of website design. The contents of the site are divided into a series of moveable vignettes (as shown below), all functioning on their own grids and adding fluidity and playfulness.

Client: Candy Chiu
Design: Candy Chiu
Grid Properties: Appropriation of previous technological styles

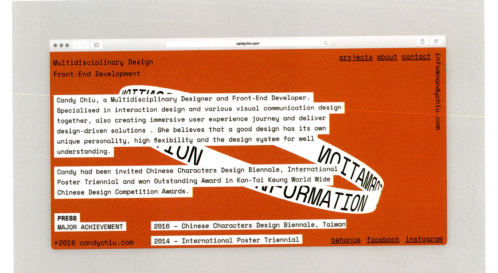

Appropriation

Appropriation

Orientation

One of the key differences between the digital and print environments is the page size that can be used. While a print job may be limited by the size of the paper stock and printing machines available, a digital page can have any dimension and be formed to fit the content perfectly.

The grid on a digital page can extend vertically and horizontally as far as it needs to, with subsequent pages each having a different size. On the other hand, a print publication tends to have pages of the same size. For example, a website could have a full-size page of a man standing up in portrait format with the next page having the same man lying down in landscape format, with each page having the dimensions needed to completely show the subject. Due to the specific restrictions inherent to digital formats, it is less common to see the use of angular text or broadside formats.

Horizontal
Horizontal orientation is suitable for a landscape presentation that scrolls left and right. This is evident in the example opposite, which allows a viewer to pan around a room. This orientation conveys the possibility of having many columns side by side. It also presents a wide potential grid, which can be scrolled horizontally.

Vertical
Vertical orientation is suitable for a portrait presentation that scrolls up and down, allowing a viewer to descend down a body of information. This offers the possibility of having a limited amount of very long columns, similar to a traditional editorial grid.

Descending
A descending orientation sees layers of design elements and content building upon one another, eventually reaching the final look of the design.

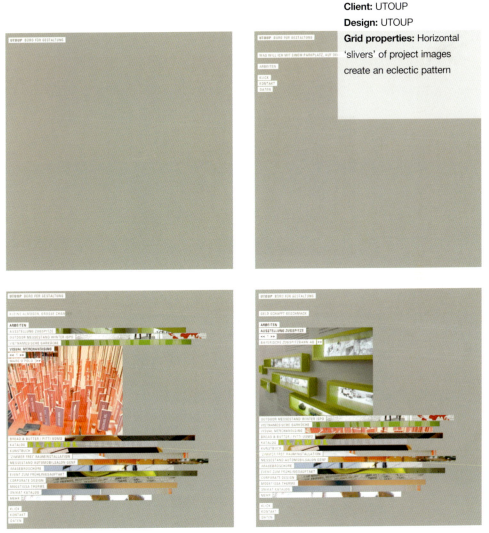

Client: UTOUP
Design: UTOUP
Grid properties: Horizontal 'slivers' of project images create an eclectic pattern

Orientation

UTOUP

This website for German design group UTOUP uses a series of horizontal image slivers or windows to generate a sense of intrigue. The juxtaposition of the images hints at the work below. Once expanded, the showcased work reads as a series of horizontally scrolling images.

Winebar Neumeister / Restaurant Saziani Stub 'n

Shown is a website that brings together two businesses, Neumeister winery and the 3-cap-restaurant Saziani Stub'n, in the picturesque municipality of Straden, Austria. A grid, reminiscent of a restaurant menu, is used as a digital platform to present the mix of aspirational images reflecting the sense of care and craft, and subtle, understated typography.

Client: Winebar Neumeister/
Restaurant Saziani Stub'n
Design: Studio Bruch
Grid Properties: Translation
of print form characteristics

Siobhan Davies Dance

This website for Siobhan Davies Dance uses a vertical structure to create order and add a dynamic element, reflecting the nature of the site. The main 'landing' page uses a simple three-column structure (above) to direct viewers to the appropriate part of the site. Once in a sub-section, as shown on the facing page, the vertical theme is used to create a sense of playful pace, with images and text placement reflecting the theme of dance.

Client: Siobhan Davies Dance

Design: Bullet Creative

Grid properties: Vertical strips containing images and text create a dynamic, yet structured website

One of the UK's leading dance companies Siobhan Davies Dance develops and presents the distinctive choreographic voice of its founder and director.

> Home
> Siobhan Davies Dance works
> Projects for schools & young people
> Side by Side
> News

Siobhan Davies Studios host a rich mix of events, classes, workshops and exhibitions designed to stimulate both the mind and the body.

> Home
> Events and exhibitions
> Dance classes
> Complementary therapies
> News

Siobhan Davies Relay broadcasts digital exchanges of ideas about dance and choreography, including the recently launched Siobhan Davies Replay.

> Home
> Siobhan Davies Replay
> Conversations on Making
> Parallel Voices 2010
> Exhibitions archive

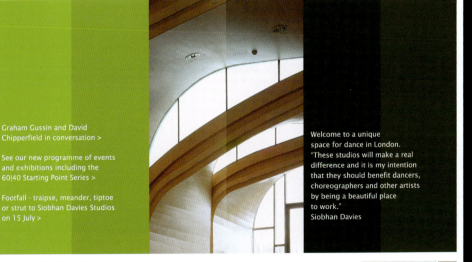

SIOBHAN DAVIES STUDIOS

Home
Classes
Therapies
Events & Exhibitions
Space Hire
About

News
Contact
Mailing List
Siobhan Davies Dance
Siobhan Davies Relay

Graham Gussin and David Chipperfield in conversation >

See our new programme of events and exhibitions including the 60|40 Starting Point Series >

Footfall - traipse, meander, tiptoe or strut to Siobhan Davies Studios on 15 July >

Welcome to a unique space for dance in London. "These studios will make a real difference and it is my intention that they should benefit dancers, choreographers and other artists by being a beautiful place to work."
Siobhan Davies

Orientation

Search | Go

Mailing list | Join

Unthink
Unthink's website uses a vertically oriented format to showcase their work. The grid on the homepage creates a montage of eclectic elements, leading through to expanded pages of project images and text.

Client: Unthink

Design: Unthink

Grid properties: Vertically oriented grid showcasing work to its maximum visual impact

Art Direction
Book
Brochure
Exhibition
Identity

Illustration
Invitation
Logos
Magazine
Music

Poster
Skateboard
Stationery
Web
About Us

A Space For Learning   ×

Irish Architecture Foundation / Exhibition / Identity

A project which teamed up architects with transition year students to examine how schools could be improved and culminated in an exhibition in the NCAD Gallery. The bespoke typeface we created for the accompanying book was used on exhibition signage. Bold window graphics created awareness on the street and inside printed cardboard boxes held info about the exhibits.

Share This on Facebook / Twitter

Orientation

Layering and tactility
We often think of online grids as being linear in nature, with one page opening another.

Blackbook Publications (above, facing page and following pages)

In this design for Blackbook Publications, Lundgren+Lindqvist adopted a design strategy to introduce layering and tactility to the website. Hands are used to add a tactile, human element indicating the tactile nature of the books. All books were photographed with hands in the shots with the exception of the covers that are presented in isolation.

Tactile graphic elements and patterns have been introduced to add a direct connection to the product and to make for a more engaging experience.

Client: Blackbook Publications
Design: Lundgren+Lindqvist
Grid Properties: Layering
of elements and tactility
in web design

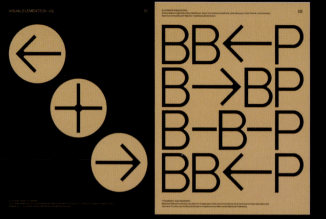

BOOKS ARTISTS BLOG PROFILE CONTACT
NEWS FACEBOOK INSTAGRAM (#BLACKBOOKPUBLICATIONS)

+ MANY VISITORS AT SUPERMARKET ART FAIR TODAY. STOP BY OUR TABLE IF YOU ARE AROUND.
— PUBLIC RELEASE OF 'WOUNDS', THE NEW BOOK BY SIMON BERG.

A collection of still lives printed in a delicate
format with a debossed title and transparent
foiling, bound with three metal staples.
The book is also available in a signed and limited edition of 15. Each one comes with a
unique can, depicting an image from the book.
The book is now available in the webshop.
Please get in touch with any questions.

+ BLACKBOOK PUBLICATIONS AT SUPER
+ COME VISIT US AT FOTOGRAFISKA MU
O NEW SIGNE VAD EXHIBITION AT GALLE
+ BLACKBOOK PUBLICATIONS AT THE SW   RG.
+ LOTTA TÖRNROTH EXHIBITION AT CEN
O JENS FRIIS WITH SIMON BERG AT LAND
O BLACKBOOK PUBLICATIONS ARE NOW   AL THIS WEEKEND.
+ LAST TWO COPIES OF 'ALBUM' BY KAL
O BUY THE LAST TEN COPIES OF (III) BY S
+ BLACKBOOK PUBLICATIONS AT THE PH
+ JOIN US AT THE OPEN AIR BOOK F
+ LOTTA TÖRNROTH AND SIMON BERG I
+ THIS WEEKEND YOU WILL FIND US AT LIBROS MUTANTES MADRID ART BOOK FAIR.
+ BLACKBOOK PUBLIACTIONS AT TEXTIVAL IN GOTHENBURG THIS SATURDAY.
+ AGNES THOR'S 'AS THE RIVER RUNS', NOW IN AVAILABLE IN THE WEBSHOP.
+ JUXTAPOZ MAGAZINE: NEW FEATURE ON 'AS THE RIVER RUNS' BY AGNES THOR.
O BOOK SIGNING: ,AS THE RIVER RUNS', BY AGNES THOR. WELCOME.
+ BLACKBOOK PUBLICATIONS AT BOK OCH BILD, 2015.
O BLACKBOOK PUBLICATIONS AT LONDON ART BOOK FAIR, 2015.
+ TWO PARTS OF THE TATTOO FROM SIMON BERGS BOX (III) AT LANDSKRONA FOTOFESTIVAL.
+ WE ARE LANDSKRONA FOTOFESTIVAL 2015

Album

ALBUM
BY KALLE SANNER

The photographs of Kalle Sanner are contem-
plative studies of light and its constant transformation. The act of photographing is more
central than the subject and location.
There is a painterly quality in Kalle Sanner
photographs and the darkest ones recall Mark
Rothko's saturated and rust-red images. He
dwells not in the gloom but allows light to
guide him through the rooms... If photographs
are drawings in light you could say that Kalle
Sanner's portrait of light actually captures
the essence of photography."
– Excerpt from catalogue, Dragana Vujanovic,
Curator Hasselblad Foundation

PUBLISHED: 2010
EDITION: 300
PRINT: OFFSET PRINTED & STAPLE BOUND
ISBN: 978-91-978317-2-7

€18

BUTIKEN
BY JOHAN MARKUSSON

At first sight it might look rigid, but in the en-
counters between customers and employees,
there are humorous and poetic elements.
This fictive story takes place in a store where
the customers are being helped at the counter.
Employees organize goods for the customers,
utilising carts and packing lists.

FORMAT: 135 × 220 MM
EDITION: 200
PUBLISHED: 2015
ISBN: 978-91-978317-7-2

BOOKS ARTISTS BLOG PROFILE CONTACT

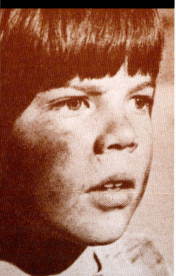

PASSING THROUGH A DARKROOM
BY ANNIKA VON HAUSSWOLFF

'Passing Through a Darkroom', by Annika von
Hausswolff, is a staple-bound artist book, signed
by the artist, both with a signature and a
fingerprint. The book was made and published
in 2017, specially for the exhibition 'Revision',
held at Konstepedemin in Gothenburg. Made
available in a limited edition of 500 copies.

PUBLISHED: APRIL 2017
EDITION: 500, SIGNED AND NUMBERED
PRINT: OFFSET PRINTED & STAPLE BOUND
ISBN: 978-91-978317-7-2

A-series paper sizes
ISO metric standard paper size based on the square root of two ratio. The A0 sheet (841 x 1,189mm/33.1 x 46.8 in) is one square metre and each size (A1, A2, A3, A4, etc.) differs from the next by a factor of either 2 or 0.5.

Active page area
An area on the page that attracts the eye.

Alignment
Text location within a text block in the vertical and horizontal planes.

Anatomy of a page
The different structures that organize and present information on a page.

Angular grid
A grid where text and image elements are used at an angle.

Asymmetrical grid
A grid that is the same on recto and verso pages, which typically introduces a bias towards one side of the page (usually the left).

Axis
The invisible line of balance or stress that runs through a design.

B-series paper sizes
ISO metric standard paper size based on the square root of two ratio. B-sizes are intermediate sizes to the A-series sizes.

Baseline grid
A graphic foundation composed of lines on which a design is constructed.

Binding
Any of several processes that holds together the pages or sections of a publication using stitches, wire, glue or other medium.

Body copy
Text that forms the main part of a work.

Broadside
Text presented to read vertically rather than horizontally.

Captions
Text that describes or names graphic elements.

Column
A vertical area or field into which text is flowed.

Composition
The combination of text and image elements to create a design.

Compound grid
A grid combining columns and modules.

Cross-alignment
A typographical hierarchy where the different levels share a common relationship, and can be aligned in the same grid.

Display type
Large and/or distinctive type intended to attract the eye and designed to be viewed from a distance.

F-shaped reading pattern
A reading pattern produced by attempting to quickly draw information from a website.

Fibonacci numbers
A series of numbers discovered by Fibonacci where each number is the sum of the preceding two. They are important because of their link to the 8:13 ratio, also known as the golden section.

Floating or translation plates
With a floating plate, all text that is to be translated is placed in one colour, usually a single black, but it could be any colour. This is then overprinted onto the colour bank for each language. This effectively reduces the number of plate changes, and therefore the cost, involved.

Fold (web page)
An imaginary line signifying the limit of what can be seen on a

Web page before having to scroll down.

Folios
Page numbers.

Format
The size/proportions of a book or page. This includes the print finishing and binding of the piece.

Grouping
Bringing together or gathering units or blocks of related information.

Gutter
The space that comprises the fore-edge or outer edge of a page, which is parallel to the back and the trim. It is the centre alleyway where two pages meet at the spine. It could also mean the space between text columns.

Head margin
The space at the top of the page; also called top margin.

Hierarchy
A logical, organized and visual guide for text headings, indicating levels of importance.

Horizontal alignment
The lining up of text in a field, on its horizontal plane. Text can be aligned centre, range right, range left, or justified.

Hyphenation
The insertion of a hyphen at the point where a word is broken in a justified text block.

Image
A visual element (e.g. photograph, diagram, drawing).

Intensity
Refers to how crowded a design or spread is.

International Paper Sizes
A range of standard metric paper sizes developed by the ISO.

Inverted pyramid
A style of presenting information in which the most important information leads a piece,

followed by further information decreasing in importance.

Justified
Text that is extended across the measure, aligning on both left and right margins.

Juxtaposition
The placement of different elements side by side in order to establish links or emphasize contrast.

Kerning
The spacing between letters or characters.

Layout
The placement of text and images to give the general appearance of the printed page.

Letter spacing
The distance between the letters of a word.

Locking to a grid
Fixing text to the baseline grid so that the grid determines spacing between text lines.

Marginalia
Text matter that appears in the page margins.

Margins
The spaces surrounding a text block at the sides, top and bottom of a page.

Measure
The width, in characters, of a page or text column.

Modernism
'Form follows function' is a phrase attributed to the architect Louis Sullivan. It succinctly captures the notion that the demands of practical use be placed above aesthetic considerations in design. This ideological approach proposed doing away with superfluous adornment in order to focus principally on usability.

Module-based grid
A grid composed of an array of modules or fields, usually squares.

Narrative
The unfolding story in a design which is a product of the relationship between its different elements.

Negative leading
This occurs when text is set with a point size greater than the leading to produce tight line spacing.

Orientation
The plane or direction in which text and images are used.

Pagination
The arrangement and numbering of pages in a publication.

Passepartout
A frame or border around an image or other element.

Passive page area
An area of a page that does not attract the eye.

Perimeter
The outer edge of a page or spread.

Proportion
The scale relationship between page elements.

Pull quotes
A section of text that is isolated and enlarged to create a separate, highlighted design element.

Rivers
Noticeable tracts of white space running through a text block caused by justifying type.

Rule of odds
A composition guide stipulating that an odd number of elements is more interesting than an even number.

Rule of thirds
A composition guide using a 3 x 3 grid to create active hotspots.

Scholar's margin
A column occupying the outer margin of a page, which is usually used for marginalia or writing notes related to the main body text.

Set solid
To set text with the same leading as its type size. For example, 10pt type with 10pt leading.

Symmetrical grid
A grid where the recto and verso pages mirror each other.

Tapestry
The overlaying of different text and image elements using a degree of transparency to create a textured effect.

Text block
A body of text that forms part of a design.

Thumbnail
A collection of small-scale images comprising a publication's pages. Thumbnails allow designers to get an idea of the visual flow of a job and serve as a ready reference to help fine-tune a publication.

Typographic colour
Colour blocks created by text elements as a result of font, weight and size.

Vertical alignment
Where type or text is aligned on a vertical plane within a field. Text can be arranged to align from the top, the bottom, the centre, or be justified within the text block.

White space
The unused space between design elements.

Word spacing
The space between words. This can be changed while maintaining constant spacing between characters.

x-height
The x-height of a typeface is the height of its lower-case 'x'.

Glossary

Index

Agency	Contact	Page number
3 Deep	www.3deep.com.au	98–9, 189
Andy Vella	www.velladesign.com	166–7
Bedow	www.bedow.se	7, 151–3
Bullet Creative	www.bulletcreative.com	200–1
Candy Chiu	www.candychiu.com	192–5
Crush Design		168–9
Delivered By Post	www.deliveredbypost.com	74–7
Design By Journal	www.designbyjournal.co.uk	50
Disciplina	www.cargocollective.com/disciplina	141–3
Faydherbe/De Vringer	www.ben-wout.nl	26, 59, 80–1, 82, 133, 134
Fieldwork Facility	www.fieldworkfacility.com	128–131
Gabor Palotai Design	www.gaborpalotai.com	3, 45–7, 154–5, 170–1
Grade Design	www.gradedesign.com	8, 21–3, 33, 69
Hvass & Hannibal	www.hvasshannibal.dk	122–3
Hype Type	www.hypetypestudio.com	136–9
Landor	www.landor.com	42–3
Lavernia & Cienfuegos Diseño	www.lavernia–cienfuegos.com	39
Leterme Dowling	www.counter-print.co.uk	108–9
Lost & Found Creative	www.lostandfoundcreative.co.uk	190–1
Lundgren+Lindqvist	www.lundgrenlindqvist.se	204–7
Michael Harvey	www.michaelharveyphoto.com	145
Morse Studio	www.morsestudio.com	70–1
Motherbird	www.motherbird.com.au	183–5
Mousegraphics	www.mousegraphics.gr	41
NB: Studio	www.nbstudio.co.uk	60, 106, 120–1
Ömse	www.omsestudio.com	36–7
Original Champions of Design	www.originalchampionsofdesign.com	176–9
Our Place	www.ourplace.studio	156–9
Pentagram	www.pentagram.com	15, 91, 93, 135, 147
Research Studios	www.researchstudios.com	14, 49, 88, 107, 172–5
Richard Eckersley	www.richardeckersley.net	164–5
SEA Design	www.seadesign.co.uk	125
Social Design	www.socialuk.com	73, 111
Studio Bruch	www.studiobruch.com	198–9
Studio Myerscough	www.studiomyerscough.co.uk	187
Studio Output	www.studio-output.com	17–19
Third Eye Design	www.thirdeyedesign.co.uk	29, 57, 79, 83, 87, 103, 113, 116, 117
Thirteen	www.thirteen.co.uk	63, 85, 161, 163, 180
Unthink	www.unthink.ie	51, 148–9, 202–3
UTOUP	www.utoup.com	11, 197
Voice Design	www.voicedesign.net	112
Webb & Webb	www.webbandwebb.co.uk	13, 24–5, 118, 126–7
why not associates	www.whynotassociates.com	105

Lost and Found Creative©Andrew Hussey, Creative Director, Lost and Found Creative; Morse©Morse Studio Ltd.; Grade©Grade Design Consultants Limited; Bedow©Bedow; 3 Deep©3 Deep 2012; Studio Myerscough©Studio Myerscough; Disciplina©2011 Disciplina; Vella Design©Andy Vella/Foruli; UTOUP©UTOUP; Gabor Palotai Design©Gabor Palotai Design; Landor ©2017 Landor. All rights reserved, top image on p43: photography by Thomas Dhellemes; Journal©Journal Ltd; Leterme Dowling Design: Jon Dowling, Company: Counter-Print; Hype Type Studio, Selected Works. www.hypetypestudio.com; Studio Bruch Concept and Design: Bruch, Photography: Erwin Polanc, Marion Luttenberger; Lundgren+Lindqvist: Design & Art Direction: Lundgren+Lindqvist, Photography: Kalle Sanner

We would like to thank everyone who supported us during the project – the many art directors, designers and creatives who showed great generosity in allowing us to reproduce their work. Thanks to Xavier Young for his patience, determination and skill in photographing the work showcased.